GOD'S DREAM

His plan for us

Bernard Prevost

GOD'S DREAM

His plan for us

St Paul Publications

Original title: *Le reve de Dieu sur l'humanité*
Copyright © Éditions du Centurion, Paris 1985

Translated by William Burridge WF

St Paul Publications
Middlegreen, Slough SL3 6BT, England

English translation copyright © St Paul Publications 1987
Printed by the Society of St Paul, Slough
ISBN 085439 262 9

St Paul Publications is an activity of the priests and brothers of the Society of St Paul who proclaim the Gospel through the media of social communication.

Contents

Jesus Christ today

A bunch of twelve-year-old boys and girls converged on the catechism centre. The new school year had just begun. They were good practising youngsters and had handed in their names for the week-by-week gatherings with a lady catechist for the coming year.

So, to the first gathering they come and are busy making themselves known to one another.

"Well", says the catechist, "what shall we do this year?"

There's an awkward silence. Then a girl pipes up: "Well, anyway, don't go on talking to us about Jesus Christ", she says. "Honestly, we've had as much as we can take of that. We've had nothing else for the last three years. We want to talk about the things we get puzzled about. All about our chums and the friends we make and love and the films and what we see on the tele, how we get on with our mum and dad and the teachers at school. I mean, just life, what's happening all around us".

As much as they can take about Jesus Christ! Just what idea of Christ have they got into their heads? Is it a picture of someone who lived two thousand years ago and then died and that was that? Or have they been shown the Christ who still lives on today? Was it Christ belonging exclusively to the Jewish world of ancient Palestine or Christ incarnate likewise in the very world of these twelve-year-olds themselves? Was it Christ the light and life of only the people of long ago or Christ the light and life of people right down the centuries for ever and all the time?

We must of course be acquainted with the historical Christ, Jesus of Nazareth. We must see him at that time welcoming the lowly folk, the poor, the sick, the loathed tax-collectors, the lepers and sinners, all those who were looked down on and shunned in his day. And we must see him taking their side even at the risk of falling foul of the authorities. We must see the kind of freehand he took with regard to some religious customs and narrow interpretations of the law then current.

1

But if we set out to get this picture of Christ it is not just because it offers us an interesting study of history and thought. What we are out to discover is the Spirit which animated Christ in everything he did so that we too, as true disciples, may be led by that same Spirit.

"Jesus Christ is the same yesterday and today and for ever" (Heb 13,8).

Christ's contemporaries in Palestine found it difficult to recognise in him the Messiah, the Saviour and light of the world, God incarnate in their midst.

No wonder then if nowadays we do not find it easy to see in him the light that solves the problems we are up against or to recognise in him God ever present in mankind of today being called by him to the fulness of life.

Jesus Christ our contemporary. Do we believe it? Jesus Christ living in us and facing up to the issues of today as he faced up to the queries of the scribes and Pharisees and the crowds of long ago.

We have to seek out and recognise this presence of Christ alive in us today. And that cannot be done without our thinking things out personally and praying about it.

We have to think things out if we are to get a better grasp of God's plan, what he would have mankind and each of us be.

And we must pray, so as to see how we personally fit into that plan and in order to steep ourselves in the life and Spirit of Christ as he draws us to himself.

God's dream

[as I told it to my parishioners]

"Wisdom rejoices before God always, rejoicing in his inhabited world and delighting in the sons of men". (Prov 8,31)

If we were to give free rein to our imaginations we might allow ourselves to conjure up for a moment a make-believe picture of the Holy Trinity. It would see the Father, Son and Holy Spirit saying: "If we were creatures, what kind of role would we prefer to play?"

The Father might say: "I would be a fountain, the source of being and of love and of life. A fountain for ever gushing with water, inexhaustible, unstinting. And in the waters of that fountain, as in a mirror, we would discern our own image and likeness".

Then we could imagine God smiling with delight as he creates the universe. And down the millions of succeeding years all kinds of forms of life appear and spread round the world ending up at last with mankind.

Then we imagine the Son. He watches as mankind comes into being and says: "I would like to be a man and a spouse to this mankind that springs from our creative fountain, to love mankind and unite myself with each and every member of the human race. This I would do to answer their yearning for happiness and friendship, justice and love, truth and beauty. And I would nurture them with our own life so that they may have life to the full, to make them resemble us and grow in beauty, free from stain and wrinkle and every imperfection, to make humanity share our joy so that their joy may be perfect".

Then in the womb of the Virgin Mary was celebrated this espousal of the Son with humanity. Never could there be a closer link.

And the Word was made flesh.

Then the Holy Spirit says: "As for me, I would be a fire,

3

the flame of love and light, a flame that enlightens the mind and warms the heart, a flame to envelope and purify everything it reaches, a fire that transforms even the hardest metals into itself, a flame of happiness, a display of light to celebrate espousals, a flame that nothing can ever extinguish".

Then the Holy Spirit breathed forth his fire to fill the universe. And the flame leapt up and enveloped the minds and melted the hearts of all who gladly exposed themselves to it.

And so after myriads of ages go by, the fulness of created beings melts in with the fulness of the Divinity and the God of love shall be all in all.

Where do we come from and where are we going?

"For he has made known to us in all wisdom and insight the mystery of his will, according to his purpose which he set forth in Christ as a plan for the fulness of time, to unite all things in him, things in heaven and things on earth". (Eph 1,9–10)

Scientists have tried to unravel the mystery of the origins of man and popularised evolution.

Nowadays they tell us that in the course of hundreds of millions of years living beings have progressively evolved until, some four million years ago, the very first "men" were produced.

Although they were still very primitive indeed — for example, the Austral — they could rightly be labelled "men" since they showed signs of intelligence. For instance, they were able to make tools from stones. And then another million years on we find still stronger claimants to the label "man": Neanderthal Man and others.

These "cave men", our ancestors, lived precarious lives, still closely allied to an animal, brute existence. Whilst it is true, as we have said, that they showed signs of intelligence, which is evidence of the beginning of a spiritual quality, this was far from being able to control all their primary instincts and these held sway over them.

Alongside these statements of the scientists, the theologians have given us a fresh understanding of creation. They see the creative work of God not simply as a once-and-for-all act. By way of comparison: a watchmaker makes a watch and once that's done the watch functions with no further help from the maker. But God is not a "maker" but the creator, and the impact of the creator on the creature never ceases. God's creative action goes on all the time, throughout evolution and in the very being and life of creatures. Theologians invented the term "evolutional creation" to describe this fact. What it amounts to is that the long, long, evolution of living beings is

5

constantly activated from within by the creative power of God.

When it comes to grasping what this evolution is really all about we have to turn to Christian revelation. Science may be able to describe what goes on in the step-by-step evolutionary process, but it is faith rooted in the Word of God that discloses the innermost why and wherefore of evolution.

So what does the Word of God tell us? It tells us that throughout the long evolution of living beings, all the time the creator had in view the production of a human being who would be perfectly made to his own (God's) image and likeness, a human being in whom he could see his own reflection, whom he could love with an infinite love and who would respond in an infinite manner to that love. It would be a being who would be at one and the same time completely endowed with free will and self-mastery and filled with the divinity and animated by its spirit: a human being who would think the thoughts of God, love as God loves and be the crowning being and achievement of all the rest of creation together. To put it another way, even before the first men ever appeared on earth, God had in mind Jesus Christ. It was with Jesus Christ in view and for Jesus Christ, and in order ultimately to lead up to him and gather all things together in him, that God created the world and that he perpetuates his creative power in it throughout the ages. As St Paul tells us, it is in Christ that all things were made. In God's plan Christ is the origin and accomplishment of all things, the First and the Last, Alpha and Omega, so that in him the fulness of creation is called to meet the fulness of the Divinity in love (Eph 1,3–14; Col 1,12–20; 1 Cor 15,27–28; Rev 22,13). This insight of our Christian faith throws light on the findings of both science and history.

Starting from the very first man, from indeed the first instant when the first glimmer of human intellect was sparked off, humanity has moved slowly forward on its long journey of progress. There was the long drawn out breakaway from the status of the sheer beast and the isolation of individualism, gradually disclosing living intellect, communal life and freedom. . . There was the long journey from the aura of violence and barbarity to the discovery of mutual tolerance, from slavery and injustice to fraternity and solidarity, from abject penury to the realisation of the dignity of each and every one, especially of the weakest of all.

6

The paleontologists and historians have applied themselves to unravelling this long upward climb of humanity, but our faith tells us that it all took place because the risen Christ drew it on all the time, ever at work to rectify deviations and purify it and redirect it. For it is Christ who is at one and the same time the invisible driving force of all human history and its ultimate fulfilment, its final end.

This long ascent of humanity was only accomplished step by slow and faltering step, often hesitant, with many ups and downs and even lapses due to inadequacy or refusal to respond. Nevertheless Christians firmly believe that humanity will not end up in final irreversible disaster and distress but that, thanks to the risen Christ, it will ultimately enter into the glory of God, the kingdom of love and the fulness of life. That indeed is what Christ prayed for, as St John's gospel records: "Father, I desire that those whom thou hast given me, may be with me where I am . . . even as thou, Father, art in me, and I in thee, that they also may be in us . . . that the love with which thou hast loved me may be in them" (cf Jn 17).

We believe that day by day under the breath of the Spirit of God, humanity advances towards maturity. It is man's distinctive trait to be receptive to what the future may bring. He cannot immediately put his hand on what that will prove to be but all his aspirations lead him to glimpse that it can never reach fulfilment apart from God who ever draws him onwards.

Little by little men learn how to live in mutual love and peace. They bring themselves to respond to the voice of conscience. Though they may not be aware of it they are collaborating with the plan of God. The risen Christ grows within us and impregnates us with his Spirit in order to make us all, if we are only willing, sons and daughters of God.

"If we are only willing" is a key phrase. We can either give or withhold our collaboration and endeavours towards this long ascent of humanity towards spiritualisation, divinisation and a way of living permeated by love.

That ascent can be impeded by cowardice, refusal to collaborate, egoism or inertia. There may even be a reversal to slavery in new forms and a new barbarity made possible by modern scientific discoveries. By contrast, when we allow ourselves to be animated by the Holy Spirit of God, the Spirit of Jesus Christ, urging us to live in communion with God and with our fellowmen, then that same Spirit produces in us and around us his fruits of joy and peace, patience and kindliness, gentleness and self-discipline (Gal 5,22ff).

We are thus all mutually responsible for this progress of humanity towards its fulfilment; we can hasten it or block it.

This is true of those who may never have come to a knowledge of Christ. Like all Christians they also are meant to be willingly animated by the spirit of love, solidarity and communion with others: "Come, O blessed of my Father; . . . for I was hungry and you gave me food . . . I was sick and you visited me. I was in prison and you came to me . . . As you did it to one of the least of these my brethren, you did it to me" (Mt 24,34ff).

If we are mutually responsible for the progress or the backsliding of humanity, it is our solidarity in the risen Christ that makes us stronger than all the adverse powers. The life, death and resurrection of Christ is our guarantee that in the end love will triumph over all and God's plans will prevail.

Past, present and future, all merge into one, all making up both the long history of man and the unfolding of God's plans as the work of his hands. The history of the world tells the story of events for which we are fully responsible. But, at the same time, deep within these events and decisions, there is the story of God's action, the story of Jesus Christ walking at the head of humanity, "setting the pace", drawing all things to himself in order to lead them on to the Father.

That is the hope which inspires us. The image we have of the end of the world is not that of a cosmic catastrophe but of an accomplishment, a supreme crowning of it all.

True enough, as Vatican II tells us, "we know neither the moment of the consummation of the earth and of man nor the way the universe will be transformed. But we are taught that God is preparing a new dwelling and a new earth in which righteousness dwells, whose happiness will fill and surpass all the desires of peace arising in the hearts of men. . . When we have spread on earth the fruits of our nature and our enterprise — human dignity, brotherly communion and freedom — according to the command of the Lord and in his Spirit, we will find them once again, cleansed this time of the stain of sin, illuminated and transfigured, when Christ presents to his Father an eternal and universal kingdom of truth and life, a kingdom

of holiness and grace, a kingdom of justice, love and peace"
(Gaudium et Spes 39).

*   *   *

Lord, we thank you for showing us what, in your eyes, true progress is.

The world of commerce grooms us to identify progress with whatever helps to make life more smooth running, like all the technical inventions which are for ever transforming the daily round of life and working conditions and international communications.

But the danger of all this material progress is that it can lead us astray, so that we forget what true human progress is, the kind of progress which finds an outlet in greater solidarity among nations, a greater drive both for justice and brotherhood and against every form of evil — violence, war, deceit, pride and suppression.

To sum it all up, the law of true human progress and the law of your kingdom, the law of love, meet together: "Thou shalt love the Lord thy God . . . thou shalt love thy neighbour as thyself".

Lord, in the light of this I am forced to confess how slow my own progress is, as well as that of humanity at large. The latest high-speed train may well break all records but it is not that kind of thing that ensures the advancement of your kingdom. In any case I am not answerable for the high-speed train! But I am responsible for your kingdom here on earth. That is my concern and the concern of each and everyone of us.

It is not a matter of denying how useful material progress can be, especially when, for example, it is used to improve the fate of developing countries or deprived sections of society. But even then material progress is a means and not an end in itself.

Material progress is necessary to help us to be more fully human beings, better able to foster our growth, our life and the life of the whole world. But we run the risk of being shackled by it if we allow ourselves to think of it as the be-all and end-all of our existence.

Lord, help us never to forget that you have made us for yourself and that our hearts will ever be restless until they rest in you, filled with your life and love and thus also ever open to our fellowmen.

Lord, may I never prove to be a dead weight in the long ascent of humanity towards its assigned end; still less may I never drag it downwards.

Teach me, rather, in all the reality of my present situation, how I can become something of a driving force in that onward march of my fellowmen towards the true life, the life that spells communion amongst all in fraternal love. To achieve this I need to be ever on the look-out, ready to take myself in hand, to work, to forge ahead.

But I must do all this in the light of your Spirit, with a sense of mutual respect, solidarity and peace. Thus will your kingdom come and your loving plans for man be realised.

God's plan

"My Father is working still and I am still working"   (Jn. 5,17)

When an architect wishes to put up a building he makes careful plans, leaving nothing to chance.

It may sometimes happen that as work proceeds unforeseen circumstances arise, such as defects in the site or in the materials at hand or troubles with manpower, and these call for slight alterations in the plans. But by and large he sticks to the original plan.

God, the creator of the universe and of man, has likewise a plan. It is one that takes time to carry out because he does not wish to do it all on his own. He calls us to carry it out with him. We are at one and the same time his workforce and the living materials at his disposal. But we are a workforce that does not always come up to his expectations and materials that fail to answer to his specifications.

The fact is that God has created us with free will. We are able to choose, to take our own decisions, to comply or refuse to comply. God took an enormous risk in giving us free will by which we either give ourselves to him or turn a deaf ear to his wishes. He risked seeing us use our free will entirely for our own satisfaction, usurping his prerogative. "You will be like God" (Gen 3,5). The risk is such that we could hamper and even block the fulfilment of his plans.

God decided the risk was worth taking because his plan for mankind was geared to a response of love, a plan that could only be fulfilled by a workforce motivated by his own Spirit, working willingly and out of love and not like some preprogrammed computer.

Truly God has wished that his undertaking should be ours as well as his, even though that would entail patiently, enduringly, compassionately putting up with our inertia.

Lord, I recognise how utterly slow I am in responding to your call and how inert and unmalleable I am. You constantly encounter in me my egoism, my laziness, my negligence, self-satisfaction, inanity. But you never give up, because you take pride in lifting up the fallen, curing our ills, forgiving our faults and setting us once more on the right path. The patience you show us is the surest proof of your power and your love.

From all this we clearly conclude that Christianity is not primarily an abstract doctrine unrelated to everyday reality nor a belief in a God who is distanced from us in his heavenly home and looks down on us from afar.

No; Christianity is first and foremost an historical fact, the story of God at work all through the history of mankind.

That comprises the story of mankind from prehistoric times right to today, the history of peoples and civilisations, history as written down by historians, with their interpretation of cause and effect of the events they record.

But behind this history of mankind or enshrined within it are the essential facts, and it is by faith that they are detected. Thus we find it is God who creates, God who makes his impact felt, God who is at work. Christianity is the history of the universe and of mankind seen with the eyes of faith, unfolded in the sight of God, revealed in the Bible. "When we seek the human or natural explanation of a fact we can find it", says a modern theologian, "but that does not rule out seeking and sometimes finding the divine reason for it". History is a holy thing.

Lord God, you are present in the unfolding of the history of mankind. That does not mean that you bring everything about directly and exclusively by yourself as though we were just puppets in your hands. What it does mean is that you did not create the world without having a precise objective in view. The story of the world, our history, is not a mere game of chance nor a matter of blind destiny.

Your objective, Lord, in creating the universe and mankind — and you proceed with our creation day after day and from moment to moment — is to make us share, one and all, in your very own divine life, and that for our happiness, for you are love itself, and for your glory, for you find joy in sharing with us the fulness of your life.

God never ceases to act in that manner, "My Father is working still", said Jesus. The work of God is to cause mankind to progress towards this objective: the gathering together of all men in Jesus Christ, their communion in the filial love of the Father and fraternal love for one another, their divinisation in unity. "That they may all be one; even as thou, Father, art in me, and I in thee".

That is what the definitive achievement of God's work is to be. And since we are created with that aim in view, it follows that the success of God's plan will be identified with the perfect and genuine success of our lives.

In the unfolding of God's plan one can distinguish three great phases: the Old Testament times, Christ's time on earth up to his resurrection and ascension and lastly the age of the Church and the Holy Spirit, that is to say, the time in which we live awaiting the return of Christ in his glory at the end of time (the 'parousia').

Lord God, we give you thanks for this loving plan hidden for all ages in you and which you have set forth in Christ: to unite all things in him, things in heaven and things on earth. Despite appearances, life in this world has a meaning. And so has the life of each one of us. For you know each one of us personally and count on us to collaborate with you. Whether or not your plan of love succeeds as fully as possible may be depends on each single one of us.

Thank you, Lord, for having chosen us. Thank you for having revealed to us the mystery of your love.

The Old Testament phase

"Hear, O Israel: The Lord our God is one
Lord. You shall love the Lord your God
with all your heart, and with all your
soul, and with all your strength... You
shall love your neighbour as yourself".
(Deut 6,4ff)

When anyone opens the Bible for the first time one cannot make head or tail of it. So many marvellous things happen and so many miracles! It shows a God who is for ever speaking to Abraham, Moses and the prophets. What can it all mean?

The Bible is the story of a little nation of long ago, the Jewish people. Throughout its history God was present all the time, ever active, occupied in furthering his plan for the world, just as we believe him to be present and active everywhere and in the conscience of every human being. But this story, which the Bible tells, was written by believers spelling out in clear terms the insights of their faith. The Bible then is precisely the story of that people seen with the eyes of faith.

The Old Testament is the story especially of God's patient endeavour to instruct this people whom he had chosen, rebuking, rectifying and setting them off time and again on the right path.

The Bible is the story of the activity of God and the cooperation of his people. That cooperation was never perfect, sometimes indeed negative and at other times nothing short of marvellous.

God portrays himself in all this as a father bringing up his children. In Hosea, for instance, we read of God saying: "It was I who taught Ephraim to walk, I took them up in my arms; but they did not know that I healed them. I led them with cords of compassion, with the bands of love . . . I was to them like a father lifting up his babe close against his cheek".

But his child is listless. What then will God do, abandon him or pardon him? "My people are bent on turning away from me. . . How can I give you up, O Ephraim? . . . My heart recoils within me, my compassion grows warm and tender. I will not execute my fierce anger . . . for I am God and not man" (cf Hos 11).

Men take revenge but God is patient and forgiving. "I will heal their faithlessness; I will love them freely . . . I will be as dew to Israel; he shall blossom as the lily, he shall strike root as the poplar; his shoots shall spread out; his beauty shall be like the olive, and his fragrance like Lebanon" (Hos 14,4–6).

It all began with Abraham. Impelled by the Spirit of God and probably at the same time by considerations rooted in history and to do with family affairs, Abraham leaves his country and comes to Palestine. Little does he suspect that his move is the first step towards the "gathering into one the children of God who are scattered abroad" (Jn 11,52). True enough, the growth to come is only beginning to germinate, but it is without doubt the starting point of the future of the people of Israel whom God has chosen and to whom he reveals himself. "I will make nations of you. . . And I will establish my covenant between me and you and your descendants after you throughout their generations for an everlasting covenant . . . I will multiply your descendants as the stars of heaven and as the sand which is on the seashore . . . and by your descendants shall all the nations of earth bless themselves" (Gen 17,6–7; 22,17–18).

Jews, Christians and Muslims alike would think of Abraham as the father of those who believe.

Centuries later the Hebrew people, driven by famine, took flight into Egypt where they were progressively reduced to slavery by Pharaoh and condemned to forced labour. But could God tolerate that his children should be oppressed by another nation and that one category of people should be the slaves of another?

The distinctive characteristic of man, created by God, is freedom, which means that he is able to take his own decisions, lead his own life and willingly make himself responsible for those around him and show solidarity with them.

Thus God said to Moses: "I have seen the affliction of my people . . . and have heard their cry . . . Come, I will send you that you may bring forth my people" (Exod 3,7.10).

And the whole saga of the flight from Egypt, the Exodus as it is called, stamped its mark indelibly on the faith of Israel. It is summed up in this profession of faith which we read in Deuteronomy: "A wondering Aramaean was my father; and he went down into Egypt and sojourned there, few in number; and there he became a nation, great, mighty and populous. And the Egyptians treated us harshly, and afflicted us, and laid upon us hard bondage. Then we cried to the Lord the God of our Fathers, and the Lord heard our voice, and saw our affliction, our toil, and our oppression; and the Lord brought us out of Egypt with a mighty hand and an outstretched arm, with great terror, with signs and wonders; and he brought us into this place and gave us this land" (Deut 26,5–9).

But there is something more in it than just this physical freedom to which God's sons and daughters are born. During the long journey through the desert the Hebrew people grumbled to Moses about being hungry and thirsty. They asked why they had not just stayed in Egypt and faced death. They wished they were back there with their fleshpots and bread in plenty. Was it, they say, just to die that they had been brought into the desert? For two pins they would have preferred another spell of slavery and forced labour rather than face up to all the suffering involved in becoming a free people.

The process of achieving freedom never ends. We have a permanent tendency to relapse into the slavery of our bodies, sensuality, physical ease and attachment to money. Time and again we get enmeshed in these chains as the animal in us takes over.

Becoming free means becoming a person with greater liberty to be of service, to show love for others and to focus our attention on them instead of on ourselves. As Dietrich Bonhoeffer put it: "If you are out to find true freedom you must first and foremost learn how to control your senses and your propensities so that your desires and your body do not run riot and carry you off with them". It is quite impossible to sustain a genuine freedom deep within ourselves if we give way to every whim of our bodily desires. And to realise that means having to face up to a combat with ourselves day in, day out.

To take up our theme again, then, down the centuries God educated his people in the use of freedom as well as in living a life of filial confidence towards him and of fraternal relations with others.

But his chosen people were a hardheaded and stiff-necked lot. Throughout the countless vicissitudes of the few centuries in question there is a constant story of God showing them patience, picking them up when they have come to grief, warning, forgiving and setting them off again on the right road.

A further stage in their history is the captivity in Babylon, culminating in the return from captivity in the year 583 which was almost like a second exodus. The prophets of the time sang of it superbly: "Take off the garment of your sorrow and affliction, O Jerusalem, and put on for ever the beauty of the glory from God. . . Look towards the east and see your children gathered from east to west at the word of the Holy One, rejoicing that God has remembered them. For they went forth from you on foot, led away by their enemies; but God will bring them back to you, carried in glory, as on a royal throne. . . For God will lead Israel with joy, in the light of his glory" (Bar 5,1.5.9).

And from there the story goes on, a story of the waywardness of the people, of repentance, God's patience, admonitions and pardon. And in the course of all this, what becomes of God's plan for mankind and all he has done to free his people and knit them together? In human terms it often looks like failure. But the prophets, deeply religious men that they are, are constantly alert to God's manifestation in the lives of men and in all that happens in the world, and little by little they become aware that the one true God is not just the All-powerful but still more the All-loving, and that his love is not exclusively directed towards his chosen people but extends to all the peoples on earth.

Yes, God really and truly is All-loving. So much so that the only comparisons that can give some idea of the love of God for mankind are the intensity of the mutual love of man and wife and the tender love of mother for her child. "For your Maker is your husband . . . the God of the whole earth he is called. . . For a brief moment I forsook you, but with great compassion I will gather you. In overflowing wrath for a moment I hid my face from you, but with everlasting love I will have compassion on you" (Is 54,5.7). "I will betroth you to me for ever . . . in steadfast love, and in mercy. I will betroth you to me in faithfulness; and you shall know the Lord" (Hos 2,19.20).

"But Zion said, 'The Lord has forsaken me, my Lord has forgotten me'. Can a woman forget her sucking child that she should have no compassion on her son? Even these may forget, yet I will not forget you" (Is 49,14–15).

Inspired by the Spirit of God the prophets thus recall constantly that the love of God will never weaken whatever may happen. And they proclaim that, despite appearances, a "remnant" of Israel does remain faithful, and always will. Indeed, from within the people of God ever "crippled in the gait", little by little a small spiritual élite emerges, described as the "needy of the Lord".

When God wishes to bring about something really big he often makes use of feeble means, people who know how weak and small they are. He does so precisely because, acknowledging this, they put all their trust in him and place themselves entirely in his hands. The young Mary of Nazareth, in her "Magnificat", so clearly portrays the mind of such people who place themselves completely at the disposal of the Spirit of God; they know it is God who achieves everything when he makes use of them: "He looks on his servant in her lowliness; henceforth all ages will call me blessed. The Almighty works marvels for me. Holy is his name. His mercy is from age to age on those who fear him. He puts forth his arm in strength and scatters the proud hearted. He casts the mighty from their thrones and raises the lowly. He fills the starving with good things, sends the rich empty away" (Lk 1,46 — Grail version).

Thanks to Mary's assent (her "let it be to me according to your word"), humble servant of God that she is, a new phase in God's plan is about to begin.

*   *   *

Teach me, Lord, to see the story of my life and the happenings that affect me in the light of faith. Teach me to see in them the traces of your presence, the echoes of your voice calling to me and the signs of your ever-active love.

Are you perhaps telling me as you told Abraham: Leave your country — your mediocre outlook on life, some particular habit, something to which you cling and which shackles your progress?

Or in your words to Moses do you say: I have seen the plight of my people. Go, for I send you to deliver them. Do you not see what is happening at the present time? The men and women subjected to hunger, enslaved in sub-human conditions and intolerable injustice? I want my sons and daughters to be free, enabled to lead their own lives. What are you prepared to do for them. Go! I shall be with you.

Teach me, Lord, how to bring true freedom to life within me. The calls my body makes on me are confusing, they appeal to what is best and worst in me, and they too readily pervade my thoughts. Teach me how to be a free person, master of myself and thereby totally unhampered to do what you expect of me. And what does "what you expect of me" imply? Surely, amongst other things, it means being part of that "remnant" of which the prophets spoke and about which the Virgin Mary sang in her "Magnificat".

As things are we Christians get the impression that we are becoming a minority. This exposes us to the danger of just letting things drift, falling in with the kind of talk and behaviour that goes on around us.

Lord, teach me to be all the more faithful and ready to serve, the more your Church is discountenanced and impoverished.

Second phase:
Christ's life on earth

*"In many and various ways God spoke of old to
our fathers by the prophets; but in these last days
he has spoken to us by a Son, whom he appointed
the heir of things".*   (Heb 1,1)

Jesus Christ comes to inaugurate a new and definitive phase in
the unfolding of God's plan.

God who is love comes, as it were, to graft himself on to
humanity as a means of communicating his own life to it and
transforms it, transfiguring it from within.

Jesus, the Son of God, is "grafted", so to speak, on to our
human nature by becoming incarnate and born of the Virgin
Mary. A new humanity is born with him and begins to grow, a
humanity of sons of God and a brotherhood, called to live of
God's life and love. It is truly, then, a divinised humanity and
a new creation.

But this was all brought about with supreme "tact", for God
always respects man's free will and never coerces anyone. Thus
he waited for Mary's humble consent, "Behold, I am the handmaid of the Lord. Let it be to me according to your word".

Jesus of Nazareth, then, is the eternal Son of God who
assumes a mode of human existence. He is truly, genuinely, man
and reveals to us the ideal man envisaged by God.

His is no make-believe human life. Day by day he experienced
for himself what our life amounts to, discovering in the daily
round of life the joys and sufferings it entails. In "coming down
from heaven" the Son of God lost nothing of his divine identity,
but he foregoes for the span of his life on earth the attributes
of his Godhead. "Christ Jesus, who, though he was in the form
of God, did not count equality with God a thing to be grasped,
but emptied himself [of his divine existence], taking the form of
a servant, being born in the likeness of men" (Phil 2,6–7).

In his human body and soul Jesus experienced all the fatigue
and suffering we undergo, the suspension and fear and anxiety,

the feelings of affection, joy, sadness, anger, surprise and indignation which are part and parcel of our lives.

Jesus is the perfect man. His perfection comes from his being unreservedly orientated towards God and totally filled with the Spirit of God, the Spirit of love which motivates him ceaselessly. He achieves in himself the ideal man envisaged by God from all eternity, and precisely from man's first moments on earth. In creating Adam God had Christ in view. So it is that Jesus reveals to us in his own person and through all the circumstances of his life the ideal way planned by God.

At the same time Jesus is truly God. Both by the way he lives and what he says he comes to reveal the true God, his Father.

He is the perfect image of the invisible God. The face of Christ the man reveals to us the invisible face of God the Father. Jesus Christ mourning for the widow of Nain is God who weeps for our human sufferings.

Christ welcoming and embracing the little children is God who regards each one of us with tenderness.

Christ who cures the sick, lifts up the fallen, forgives and inspires new hope and courage is God who does all these things.

The way Christ sees and assesses things is the way God sees and assesses them. His preferences reveal God's preferences. Christ, "loving his own to the very end", reveals that God our Father loves us to the very end. For has he not said: "My Father and I are one"?

In the act of revealing himself as the ideal man and true God, Christ proclaims by the same token the ideal world God had in view. Using the language of his time, Christ called it "the kingdom of God".

The kingdom of God is not a given territory nor a political administrative entity. The kingdom of God is present when one lives and acts in the filial love of God and the fraternal love of our brethren of the human race. The kingdom of God is present when we make ourselves one with the least ones of this world, when we forgive others or share what we have with them.

The kingdom of God is then a new outlook on life, a new way of living it and a new pattern of behaviour. It means living the same life as God in the manner Christ lived it.

Left to ourselves that is not possible. But that is what is held out to us. The kingdom is a gift of God. It is up to us to embrace it eagerly.

Christ himself defined it. "I have come that they may have life and have it more fully". And what exactly is this fulness of life? Quite simply the life of God. And what precisely does that imply? To live the life of God means living by love, loving as God loves. For God is love.

But loving as God loves is not consistent with just following our likes and dislikes, or cornering things for ourselves, turning them to our personal advantage. It is not going for our self-satisfaction or swooping on to the attraction of the moment. Come to think of it, Jesus loved the lepers and there was nothing particularly attractive about them!

To love the way God loves is to go all out for what is best for others even if it means sacrificing ourselves in the process. "Greater love than this has no man, that he lays down his life for others".

The kingdom of God was fully achieved in the person of Christ and the way he lived. He had to grow up little by little in the life men lead, their relations with one another and the framework of human society. It was a slow, almost imperceptible growth, rather like the growth of a plant from the seed buried in the ground and only germinating and growing almost imperceptibly.

The kingdom of God, therefore, is a new order of things which has to embrace all human relations, social and international. It takes in every aspect of the life of man, called as he is to a gradual process of transformation which starts here and now in this world. One integral aspect of it is the struggle for justice and peace amongst nations. The kingdom of God is indeed this world of ours, but having undergone a complete cure of its ills, renewed and transfigured by the Spirit of God and working in us and for the benefit of each and every one of us.

The kingdom of God is, then, at one and the same time good news for the present and hope for the future. Thanks to Jesus Christ that kingdom is already present but it is far from being fully achieved. It is a treasure that we must not allow to slip through our fingers. We must possess ourselves of it and in order to do so we must undertake a conversion. But how worthwhile the effort is in order to opt for it and commit ourselves to pursuing it! For that ensures the achievement of what God has in view for the world and, by the same token, it is for us men the fulness of life and genuine joy.

*   *   *

Lord Jesus, because you are the Son of God I am often tempted to think of you as some kind of superman.

If you were a superman you would have stood aloof from people, you would not have wept for your friend Lazarus nor have welcomed and embraced the children who came to you. You would have been quite out of reach of the ills of mankind. But far from that, Son of God, you really and truly led a life like ours. You shared the very joys and sufferings we have, our fears and our hopes, our stirrings of anger, our indignation, our affections and our unexpected joys.

In order to reveal yourself to us you have chosen this human personality which we catch glimpses of in the Gospel, and thanks to this we discern in you the invisible face of God — God so close to us, God of love and tenderness, God who comes to meet us and fulfil our expectations beyond all measure, so true it is that we are made for him. "You have made us for yourself, Lord, and our hearts are restless until they rest in you".

Teach me, Lord, to be a person to the full, that is to say, always looking towards you. For we are made for fulness of life, love and joy which you alone can give us.

Teach me, Lord, to delight in experiencing in this world the early insights of that life, love and joy, whilst always remembering that you are calling me to rise far higher still. In your love for us you would not have us barely keep alive, nor be satisfied with petty material comforts, nor indulge in snug inertia.

No; you call us to lead a truly full life, spending ourselves for the sake of others, ever growing and maturing. You would have us discover what a joy it is to be creative and constructive, to give and to pardon and, if need be, sacrifice ourselves for others. The joy you hold out is the joy of rising above ourselves, of being at the service of the greater than ourselves, the service of your kingdom and your plan for the world.

Lord, do not let me be dazzled by the first tiny spark of life, love and joy that I encounter! Let me rather always bear in mind what you have said: "I have come that my joy may be in you and that your joy may be perfect".

The death and resurrection of Jesus

*"Jesus knew that his hour had come to depart out
of this world to the Father. Having loved his own
who were in the world, he loved them to the end"*
(Jn 13,1)

The Jewish religious authorities could not fail to react to what
Jesus taught, his reactions and the stance he took, all the more
so because in official and legal terms he was just a "lay man",
the son of Joseph and Mary of Nazareth, son of a carpenter
and a carpenter himself. He was not a priest, had no qualifica-
tions in religious studies or in anything else. Humanly speaking
he had no rights and no standing. These religious authorities,
jealous as they were of their position and prerogatives, came
to regard him with suspicion. In the end they rejected this Christ
who dared to denounce their hypocrisy, their falsehoods and
their money-grabbing. Worst of all, in their eyes he preached a
God so different from theirs, a God who welcomed sinners, pardoned them and gave them the power to grant pardon to others,
a God who loved the pagans and the foreigners and lepers,
whereas these ought all to be regarded as people suffering punish-
ment from the Almighty. He was preaching a God for whom
observance of the law of Moses and the traditions of the Fathers
took a second place to the commandment of love.

But it was not only because he readjusted the law given by
God to Moses and because he claimed to be master of the
Sabbath, that they rejected him, but because he actually claimed
to be son of God. "You", they told him, "being a man, you make
yourself God" (Jn 10,33).

Jesus had foreseen this rejection. He saw his "hour" coming,
the hour of Calvary and the cross. He did not seek it nor did
he run away from it. He did not merely resign himself to it as
to an inescapable misfortune, for had he wished he could have
avoided it, found a way round it. But Jesus did not manipulate
events. He chose freely to go forward to the very end of his
mission out of love for God his Father and in order to love his
own to the end. And this he did despite the natural human

abhorrence for suffering which he felt just as much when he had to face suffering himself as when he saw others suffer. But the whole of his life, from the day of his birth, had been one act of love and of spending himself for others. And his resurrection, whatever some might think, was to be the sign that he was the supreme victor. "O death, where is thy sting?", St Paul was to exclaim. Cost what it may, the fulfilment of God's plan was to go forward.

A whole litany could be written of the sufferings assumed on Calvary as one contemplates the three crosses. There was the pain of being treated with indifference and disdain, setbacks and despair; the innocent jostled and humiliated, the poor exploited, the innocent defamed; the wretchedness of the guilty, the criminal in revolt and the criminal begging mercy; the sick, the infirm and the elderly segregated and unloved; the champion of rights persecuted and exhausted from incessant combat. There was the cross of the father forsaken by the son, that of the mother agonising over a wayward child. The cross born by the abandoned wife, the cross of the adolescent dreaming of love and liberty.

But then one's eyes turn to the central cross alone, the cross on which Christ is crucified. Christ who takes upon himself all the sufferings of the world, Christ who is there out of sheer love, the cross where the arms are outstretched to embrace the human race and all its history, the single cross planted firmly in our earth. And from that cross a cry goes up to heaven, a cry of love and hope, the cry of the newborn in a world renewed.

How did the apostles and the first Christians understand the death and resurrection of Christ? How are we to understand the salvation brought by Christ expressed in such a statement as: "Christ has saved us by his death on the cross"?

The Jewish pattern of thought in the Old Testament inevitably dictated the way in which people conceived the death of Christ.

In the temple in Jerusalem the priests offered sacrifices of animals, sacrifices of expiation, reparation and purification. These correspond to the need to redeem oneself and one's faults and purify one's conscience, expiate one's sins, make amends for one's offence or injury against God. There were also thanksgiving sacrifices to God. In some cases the victim was divided in two, one half offered to God and burnt, the other consumed by the people. This sacred meal expressed the people's desire to unite themselves with God and communicate with him in the kind of intimacy one finds in the close circle of family life where one shares the same food and the same round of life. Most of the first Christians came from amongst the Jews and used these ideas in reflecting on the passion of Christ. In their eyes Christ's sufferings and death constituted the perfect sacrifice which once and for all rendered all former sacrifices useless. By his blood poured out for us Christ has redeemed us, purified us, expiated our faults and made perfect amends to God for our offences. Thanks to him, we were reconciled to God, our sins were forgiven and we rediscovered the friendship of God and his grace which we had lost through sin.

This way of seeing the sufferings and death of Christ is found pretty well throughout the epistles (i.e., letters) of St Peter and St Paul and even in the gospels. "It is not with silver and gold that you have been redeemed", wrote St Peter, "but by the precious blood as of the perfect spotless lamb, the blood of Christ". And St Paul says that it is Jesus Christ that God has destined to serve as expiation by his blood, through faith. This terminology was in perfect keeping with the contemporary cast of mind.

But when it comes to grasping the exact content of this language nowadays, all kinds of questions arise, like how the sufferings of Christ redeem, what is the precise meaning underlying the word redemption in its original sense of "buying back", how does the blood of Christ purify? Did it imply that God imposed suffering and shedding of blood as a condition for obtaining his forgiveness and the purchase of his grace? In that case, one further asks where in this is the resemblance with the image of God revealed by Christ throughout his life.

Christ speaks of God as the father welcoming his repentant son with open arms and laying on a feast for him the moment he returns home. Again, God is the shepherd who goes off to find the lost sheep and carries it back to the fold on his shoulders. It is God likewise telling us to forgive others seventy times seven times. How then will he not grant pardon without first demanding chastisement either of us or of some intermediary?

And furthermore, are we to think of God's justice in terms of human justice? In our law courts the judge punishes the guilty in keeping with human laws and acquits the innocent or those the court finds innocent. But does God judge by our human laws? Does he not judge rather by his own law, the law of love and mercy? For God's justice is not out to punish, still less to take revenge. It seeks only to cure, to lift up the fallen, to pardon and set us on the right path again. If one speaks of justice in God it is identified with his mercy and that love which Christ showed whenever he met sinners. By their sins they have harmed themselves, and if there is indeed a wrong to be put right, it is first of all that harm and the harm they have done to others and to the world they live in.

You might almost say that God suffers from our sins, but only in the way a father or mother suffers from the foolhardy faults committed by their child or because he is ill or suffering.

The glory of God lies not in demanding justice for himself or in vindicating his violated rights, but in curing, pardoning, rehabilitating, all out of pure benevolence. For God's design is to give us a share in his life, make us his sons by giving us a likeness to Christ; in a word, to divinise us.

Does all this mean, then, that we must rule out the idea of "sacrifice" in the sufferings and death of Christ? Not in the least. But we do have to make sure that we understand exactly what the word "sacrifice" means in both the Old Testament and the New.

Right back in the Old Testament the prophets time and again stressed that what gave value to a sacrifice was not how big the victim was or how much blood was shed but the intention of the person offering it, namely, his wish to draw nearer to God, the sincerity of his remorse for the faults he had committed, his resolve to amend his ways, in a word, his love for God.

In the writings of the prophet Amos God is recorded as exclaiming: "Even though you offer me your burnt offerings, I will not accept them . . . and the peace offerings of your fatted beasts I will not look upon. . . But let justice roll down like waters, and righteousness like an overflowing stream" (Amos 5,22.24).

And Psalm 51, addressed to God, leaves no doubt: "Thou hast no delight in sacrifice; were I to give a burnt offering, thou wouldst not be pleased. The sacrifice acceptable to God is a broken spirit; a broken and contrite heart, O God, thou wilt not despise" (Ps 51,16–17).

As we would expect, the epistles and gospels are even more concerned to make this clear. Thus Jesus, taking up a passage from Hosea, says: "I desire mercy and not sacrifice" (Mt 9,13). And the Gospel of St Mark records: "To love God with all the heart, and with all the understanding, and with all the strength, and to love one's neighbours as oneself is much more than whole burnt offerings and sacrifices" (Mk 12,33). And the Letter to the Hebrews, echoing Psalm 40, puts these words on Jesus's lips: "Sacrifices and offerings thou hast not desired, but a body hast thou prepared for me; in burnt offerings and sin offerings thou hast taken no pleasure. Then I said, 'Lo, I have come to do thy will, O God' " (Heb 10,5–7).

God, then, does not take pleasure in the immolation of victims or the pouring out of blood, and still less in human sacrifices which the Bible calls an abomination. What God does take pleasure in is hearts that repent and strive to mend their ways and hearts that are loving and merciful and that faithfully comply with his will. There you have the real meaning of sacrifice. It is what the Gospel of St John calls "worship in spirit and in truth" (Jn 4,23). St Paul calls it "spiritual worship": "I appeal to you, therefore, to present your bodies as a living sacrifice, holy and acceptable to God, which is your spiritual worship" (Rom 12,1).

In this way the whole life of Jesus and not only his death on Calvary was a sacrifice, starting with the Incarnation and his birth in Bethlehem.

His sacrifice, indeed, consisted of his whole life, inspired that it was by his attachment to the Father and stimulated by his love for mankind, his perfect lifelong fidelity to his mission, while all the time knowing the terrible plight in which it would all end. His sufferings in his passion and the shedding of his blood on the cross are purely the supreme expression of his love for us, a love which he carried to its ultimate limits.

It may well be that some people in the course of time have endured even more terrible and more prolonged sufferings, but that it is not the point. What gives Christ's sacrifice its value is not the quantity of suffering but the degree of love which motivated him to the very end.

Clearly God took satisfaction in Christ's sacrifice not by virtue of the sufferings men inflicted on him but in his unwavering love in spite of all he endured and that right on to his last breath.

It was not essential to God's plan that Christ should be rejected by the Jews and condemned to death. The rejection by his people prefigured all our rejections of him, all the times men turn from him, all their sluggishness in responding to God freely and lovingly.

Christ was the first perfect man because he was the first to love perfectly and was totally orientated towards God and towards others: the man of God and the man dedicated to others out of sheer love. His death and resurrection proves to us that a love that does not stop short at giving one's life for others has the power to shatter evil and conquer death. He offers us his Spirit in order to train us in that same love. He gives the lead to all who open themselves to him by faith and so become the new humanity, the new mankind. His death and resurrection are, so to speak, the begetting and birth of that new humanity which must grow more and more and one day bring about the realisation of God's plan for mankind. And withal, it must be remembered that all this presupposes that this undertaking is projected onwards, after life in this world.

The phase of
the Church and the Spirit

*"You shall receive power when the Holy Spirit has
come upon you; and you shall be my witnesses".*
(Acts 1,8)

Christ wished his work to continue after his life on earth. Time
and again the gospels point to what the future held in store.

For the Incarnation was not to be a mere passing stay of God
here on earth as though he just came and adopted our human
way of life for a while so as to give us his message, and then
ascend again into heaven from where he would just look down
on us to watch what happened to us. What really took place was
that after his resurrection, far from leaving the world to its
own devices, he became more deeply than ever immersed in it,
so that now he is present to everything that exists in the same
way that God is present everywhere. "I am with you always",
he declared, "to the close of the age" (Mt 28,20).

The phase of the Church and the Spirit which was ushered
in after the resurrection and ascension of Christ is, then, the
era of Christ, but more precisely, the era of the risen Christ
who carries forward his work in the world through his Church
and his Spirit incessantly from age to age. That is the phase in
which we ourselves now live.

The seed of the Church was already planted in the little group
of the twelve apostles. It was on Pentecost day that it came alive.
From that instant onwards Christ's disciples came gradually
to realise how Christ's Pasch was the indispensable and decisive
stage in the unfolding of God's plan for mankind.

St Luke's account in chapter two of the Acts of the Apostles,
with the help of symbols makes it unmistakeably clear what the
mission of the Church was to be. Its allotted task is to carry
forward the work of Christ, proclaim the kingdom of God and
gather the whole of humanity in one faith and one love. The
"devout Jews from all nations under heaven" who assembled
to hear the apostles speak to them, in each in their own

language, prefigure all the people of the world. The Good News has to be brought to all nations and peoples and races and to all cultures in every language.

The Church is thus the "new Israel", the new people of God. It is universal, no longer to be confined to a single race. That image of the people of God, traditional in the Old Testament, was taken up in the early Church, notably in the Letter of St Peter, thus: "You are a chosen race, a royal priesthood, a holy nation, God's own people, that you may declare the wonderful deeds of him who called you out of darkness into his marvellous light. Once you were no people; but now you are God's people" (1 Pet 2,9–10).

Another richly significant image, frequently used by St Paul, is that of the Church as the risen body of Christ, animated by the Spirit and destined to expand throughout the world. The Church is thus Jesus Christ continuing in existence down the centuries in every place through Christians, members of that body.

To follow one of St Paul's favourite comparisons, if the Church is the body of Christ constantly building up, then it is also a structure built by God. It is the temple of God, the City of God; and the living stones with which this is built are none other than the Christians themselves.

Another of those images used to designate the Church which is found in the Old Testament, and is taken up in the New, is that of the spouse with whom Christ wishes to be united and to share all he has with her.

Lastly, in terms of the Church as the body of Christ and Christians as its members, there is the allegory of the vine in St John's gospel where Jesus says: "I am the vine and you are the branches".

In all these comparisons the Church is clearly presented as a visible institution which is not an end in itself. Its mission is to proclaim the kingdom of God and nurture the spiritual Church which is not visible. It is totally identified with the visible body of Christ but stretches far and wide with unseen powers.

The visible Church is not destined to triumph here on earth any more than Christ triumphed in his earthly life in Palestine. If the Church is faithful to its mission, it will inescapably meet with contradiction and persecution, in a word, with its "cross". Jesus warned us not to be surprised when this happens. "The servant", he said, "is not greater than his master. If they persecuted me, they will persecute you. They will put you out of the synagogues; indeed, the hour is coming when whoever kills you will think he is offering service to God. . . But I have said these things to you, that when their hour comes you may remember that I told you of them" (Jn 15,20; 16,2.4).

The aim of the Church, then, is not its own personal triumph but furthering the fulfilment of God's plan for mankind, and it must do this with Christ's own outlook and modelling itself on his way of acting, not counting the cost and fearlessly facing the storms.

"Go out into the deep", said Jesus to Peter. And to his Church he says, do not hug the safety of the quayside, do not take shelter in a world of make-believe but make your presence felt right in amongst the life of the real world.

In the following pages of this book we shall examine all these images one by one. There is much more in them than at first meets the eye, and each has something to contribute to the total picture they build up.

Let us line them all up once more.

The Church, the new Israel and the new people of God. The Church, the body of Christ, St Paul's preferential line of thought. The Church, the living temple of God. The Church, the spouse of Christ. The vine and the branches. And then this final point: God does not limit his action in the world to the Church alone. The Spirit of God, far from being confined to the visible Church, is a wind that blows where he wills, and acts and influences everywhere. For the Spirit fills the whole of creation. In view of this we shall end with a section on the Holy Spirit "beyond-the-boundaries".

*　　　*　　　*

The Pentecost of yesteryear

Some men meet and fall to talking and get to know one another. They are a mixed bunch, total strangers, but all filled with the same Spirit — Medes, Persians, people from Mesopotamia, from around the Black Sea, from Judaea, Cappadocia, Asia, Phrygia, Pamphylia, Egypt and Libya, Romans, Jews, Cretans, Arabians . . . they are all bound for the great fraternal gathering of the human race.

Whitweek nowadays

People scattered far and wide going off for a weekend break, each man for himself. A mixed bunch, total strangers to one another. No thought for one another as each jostles through the crowd. British, Irish, Asians, French, Germans, Italians, Africans, West Indians. . . Christians, Muslims, non-believers. . . Employed, labourers, shopkeepers. All in the same crowd yet never relating to one another. Can this possibly be a repeat of the tower of Babel?

Pentecost of yesteryear come alive today

The Spirit of God is at work to break down barriers, dismantle partitions and frontiers and unravel discords. The Spirit of God urges men to come out of their secret "upper rooms" and their own petty worlds where they hide away for fear of being caught up in the current of that great Wind.

The Spirit of God urges men to meet one another, to talk the same "language" while respecting their very real differences. The Spirit of God, that mighty Wind, buffets men and makes them wake up and take notice.

Where shall our choice in all this lay? Shall we opt for the Spirit's impulse which gathers and builds or for the violence of men that scatters and destroys?

The Church: people of God

*"Behold, the days are coming, says the Lord, when
I will make a new covenant with the house of
Israel. . . I will put my law within them, and I will
write it upon their hearts; and I will be their God,
and they shall be my people".*   (Jer 31,31.33)

Vatican II made a special point of the image of the Church
as the people of God (cf. Lumen Gentium 2).

Christ's people of God do not consist of the members of one
particular race. On the contrary, all the races of mankind, with
all their languages, cultures and social levels are called to make
up this new people of God, all knit together by a single faith
and a single love.

The Gospel made this clear: the people of God — the poor, the
blind, the lame — are to be made unreservedly at home, for "the
first shall be last and the last first". The people of God must be
open to all and first and foremosst to those the world habitually
despises and writes off: the poor and the socially insignificant,
the ones overlooked, the ill-famed. And the sinners too, for the
people of God are not ready-made saints but a people made up
of sinners en route towards holiness. The Gospel parable makes
the point: the kingdom of God is like a field where good seed is
sprouting but weeds have been sown amongst it. The Church
will always have the task of purifying itself and practising
penance and striving for renewal.

The Church is not thought of first of all as an organised
hierarchy with pope, bishops and priests as its essential elements
but is defined primarily as a people where all, great and small,
are entrusted with its mission, each according to their gifts and
opportunities.

By baptism Christ has involved every Christian in his enterprise. The whole purpose is to foster the growth of the kingdom
of God within whatever level of society, family or professional
framework we find ourselves in. Our task is to work for the
sanctification of the world by being kneaded into it like the yeast
into the loaf. And once you have said sanctification, you are

necessarily talking about love, reconciliation, justice and peace. That is the spirit in which we have to clarify and orientate the social, political and even international aspects of human life in all its reality.

Baptism, then, is not a kind of passport from this world to the next but a commitment to sharing actively, and with all the other baptised persons, in the mission of the Church which is none other than the on-going mission of Christ. If a day is to come when the world is to be saved, it will not be the day when all are baptised but the day when all the baptised have become genuine Christians.

Of course the baptised and the totality of the people of God need to be cared for. That means that they need indispensably men specially assigned to help them and keep them going, give them guidance, instruction, constant encouragement and energy, and to make sure they are always united and mutually cooperative. And all that is precisely the function of pope, bishops and priests and of laymen who, increasingly nowadays, undertake certain ministries.

The advantage of this kind of picture of the Church as the people of God is that it shows that the Church does not have to be out to compete with the world at large. It does not stand apart from the world nor above the world but is well and truly in the world for the benefit of the world, revealing to people the superabundant life to which Christ calls them ("I have come that they may have life") and endeavouring to permeate and activate the social, professional, political and all other structures of life with that love with which the Holy Spirit fills our hearts.

Vatican II makes a further point. Catholics, it is true, are fully incorporated into the Church. But non-Catholic Christians, thanks to their faith in Christ and their union in the Holy Spirit, also participate in realising God's plan for mankind (Lumen Gentium 15–16).

And so do people who, although they do not believe in Christ, have a certain kind of life of faith in God. Indeed even those who do not believe in God, yet are open to his grace, must be considered as participating in a certain limited but real way in the life of the Church.

So the Church as Christ would have it is an active, dynamic people, on the move and drawing along with itself the whole mass of humanity. It is a people whose whole purpose is to foster the growth of the kingdom of God everywhere, so that, little by little, the whole world may be penetrated through and through by the Holy Spirit, the Spirit of love, justice, reconciliation and peace, and all this so that some day God's plan for mankind may be fulfilled: "That all things may be brought together under one head, namely, Christ".

*   *   *

Lord God, can it be that I have not fully understood what baptism entails? It has been so easy to think of it only as making me your child and that all I was involved in was saving my soul and getting to heaven when I die. In reality by my baptism you have enlisted me in your undertaking for the salvation and transformation of the whole world. From then on you have been counting on me to carry out industriously my special Christian role.

From within your Church teach me how to be actively inspired by your Spirit of love and to live with my Christian brethren a life in keeping with the Beatitudes, so that your people may truly be seen as a sign of that new world which Christ came to launch and which has to be extended everywhere.

Teach us to be concerned for your brethren who have had the good fortune to come to know you. Teach us how to be witnesses to Christ for them; imperfect and not very brilliant witnesses, it is true, but unmistakeable and fervent witnesses for all that.

Teach us to keep a careful watch on all the organised activities in the world today so as to detect any damage they do to the lives of our brothers and wherever possible to bond together to counteract their evil influence.

Teach us not to be wrapped up in ourselves but always to look out beyond our own little world. For the Spirit urges us "out into the deep" so that your kingdom may come and your plan for mankind may be fulfilled.

The Church: body of Christ

*"You are the body of Christ and individually
members of it".* (I Cor 12,27)

This is St Paul's favourite image of the Church. The risen Christ mystically but truly constitutes all of his disciples as his body (cf Lumen Gentium 7).

Becoming a Christian by baptism means becoming a member of his body, a member, that is, of Jesus Christ. Just as my blood is a life-stream flowing in all my members — arms, legs, face, eyes, mouth — so also my baptism has united me with Christ so that, in a mysterious way, his Spirit stimulates me and his heart is united to mine. My life is, so to speak, an extension of his own here and now, for me and for all around me: "I live, no longer I, but Christ lives in me".

But, of course, this inflowing into me of the life of Christ and his Spirit, his thoughts and his preferences does not happen automatically. I have always the option of blocking it simply because God always leaves me free to choose. At each instant of each day he waits my willing consent, just as on the day of the Annunciation he waited for the Virgin Mary's "let it be to me according to your word".

All this is what St Paul kept telling the first Christians in his letters. "As in one body we have many members, and all the members do not have the same function, so we, though many, are one body in Christ, and individually members of one another" (Rom 12,4). "For by one Spirit we were all baptised into one body . . . and all were made to drink of one Spirit" (1 Cor 12,13).

And Paul, speaking of the Church whose members we are, calls it the fulness of Christ (Eph 1,23), that is to say, Christ reaching out to the totality of his members.

It is as though, figuratively speaking, the incarnation of the Son of God in our human nature was not finally accomplished at the moment of his birth 2000 years ago but is projected down the centuries each time a human being, receiving the baptism of water and the Spirit, is joined to Christ. The risen Christ thus grows constantly, thanks to all these new members, and will not reach a full and final measure until the end of time, the day when "we all attain to the unity of faith and the knowledge of the Son of God, to mature manhood, the measure of the stature of the fulness of Christ" (Eph 4,13). Thus will Christ be in all things. The plan of God — "a plan for the fulness of time, to unite all things in Christ, things in heaven and things on earth" — will be completely realised in the "whole Christ". Then will God be all things to all men.

Several important facts follow from this union with the risen Christ seen in terms of our bodily members linked with the whole of our body. The first fact is that becoming a Christian entails conversion, a change in our lives.

God's plan is to make us share in his own life, in other words to divinise us. He planned for us to "be conformed to the image of his Son, in order that he might be the first-born among many brethren" (Rom 8,29). We are thus called to be authentic copies of Christ, thinking his thoughts, loving as he loves, and behaving as he behaves. This does not mean an automatic replica of him — that is not possible, anyway. It means that in the actual circumstances in which we live we shall be inspired and stimulated by the Spirit which inspired and stimulated him in the circumstances in which he lived.

That is why Paul, dealing with the early Christians who were so beset by their various passions, constantly reminded them that by their baptism they became members of Christ and warned them not to resist the Spirit of Christ who wished for nothing better than to pervade them and transform them. If, he told them, they went on thinking and behaving the way they had done formerly their lives would be nothing but discord, hatred, anger, rivalry, jealousy, envy. And all such things, he stressed, are at variance with the Spirit of Christ. Far from behaving like that, because they had become the sons of God they should put themselves under the influence of the Spirit of God and then their lives would be full of love, joy, peace, patience, kindness, goodness, faithfulness, gentleness and self-control.

Indeed, to become a Christian is to become a new man. It means changing over to a life activated by the love of God and of others and to everything that entails. And this conversion does not consist of one final act but has to be reiterated again and again. "Put to death therefore what is earthly in you: immorality, impurity, passion, evil desire, and covetousness. . . In these you once walked . . . but now put them all away: anger, wrath, malice, slander, and foul talk from your mouth . . . seeing that [by baptism] you have put off the old nature with its practices and have put on the new nature, which is being renewed in knowledge after the image of its creator" (Col 3,5ff).

And Paul is insistent: "Put on then", he says, "as God's chosen ones, holy and beloved, compassion, kindness, lowliness, meekness, and patience, forbearing one another . . . as the Lord has forgiven you, so you also must forgive. And above all these, put on love, which binds everything together in perfect harmony. And let the peace of Christ rule in your hearts, to which indeed you were called in one body" (Col 3,12–15).

Called as we are to holiness, we must willingly allow ourselves to be incorporated in the risen Christ and divinised by the Spirit of God and transformed by the life of Christ which flows in us like the blood in our veins throughout our body. God's great wish is to be able to detect in us the image of his Son, the cause of all his joy. We must not disappoint him.

The second fact resulting from our incorporation in Christ is that by the sheer fact of being united with the risen Christ as members of his body we are also intimately united with one another. As members of Christ we are likewise members of one another.

In the time of St Paul the first communities brought together people of many different backgrounds. There were convert Jews and pagans, high-ranking people and slaves, men and women. How difficult it was for them to understand one another, to get on together and to acknowledge that people, say, one had been accustomed to mistreat because of their race, were from now on one's brothers. So Paul drives his lesson home: "For as many of you as were baptised into Christ have put on Christ. There is neither Jew nor Greek, there is neither slave nor free, there is neither male nor female; for you are all one in Christ Jesus" (Gal 3,27).

And that is how it was to be in every Christian community in every successive epoch of history. The Church must be open to the whole wide world. If it were to confine itself to one category of people or one race or one social class it would fail to be faithful to Christ. How often, alas, one finds groups of Christians that are to all intents selective circles for the initiated only, an isolated entity, where outsiders are made to feel they don't and can't belong — the common folk, labourers, immigrants and so on.

God's plan for mankind, we must never tire of repeating, is to gather together everybody as brothers, transcending all the different things about them and making them all his sons and daughters. This fulfilment of God's loving plan cannot come about unless we lay ourselves open to being stimulated and transformd by the one Spirit of love. "I therefore beg you to lead a life worthy of the calling to which you have been called, with all lowliness and meekness, with patience, forbearing one another in love, eager to maintain the unity of the Spirit in the bond of peace. There is one body and one Spirit, just as you were called to the one hope that belongs to your call, one Lord, one faith, one baptism, one God and Father of us all, who is above all and through all and in all" (Eph 4,1–6).

The third fact is this. If the risen Christ has made all Christians the members of his body and causes his life to flow in their veins, it is because he counts on us to carry forward his undertaking, namely, his mission to the world. His task becomes our task also.

We have not been baptised for our own personal sake alone, only to make sure of our own salvation. We are baptised in order to be active, dynamic and dedicated members of the body of Christ. In the Church all Christians are responsible for the progress of the kingdom of God in the world around them.

If I am baptised, a member of Christ, living, say, in Glasgow or London or in the obscure hamlet of Slow-in-the-Uptake it is because I am meant to further the task of Christ precisely in the place where I live, or rather so that Christ can make use of me to further his mission there.

As a Christian, Christ dwells in me. I am inspired and stimulated by his Spirit in order that through me his kingdom of love, justice and peace may progress around me.

For 2000 years the Church, that is, each and every Christian, has been the privileged instrument Christ makes use of to bring his plan to fulfilment. Each and every one of us must ask himself what he can do today to foster in his very own surroundings greater tolerance and mutual understanding, reconciliation and unity.

Let us hear Paul once more writing to his Christians at Ephesus. "Christ's gifts were that some should be apostles, some prophets, some evangelists, some pastors and teachers, for building up the body of Christ ... speaking the truth in love, we are to grow up in every way into him who is the head, into Christ, from whom the whole body, joined and knit together by every joint with which it is supplied, when each part is working properly, makes bodily growth and upbuilds itself in love" (Eph 4,11–16).

It follows that we must respect one another whatever our respective functions and responsibilities may be. In our own human body all the different limbs and organs are interdependent, each needs all the others and even the weakest of them is indispensable. That, too, is how it is in the body of Christ. God wished each and every member to share in mutual concern for one another. "If one member suffers all the members suffer with him, if one member is honoured all the members share his joy". We could do well to read and meditate chapters 12 and 13 of the First Letter of St Paul to the Corinthians.

As a member of the risen Christ who lives for ever, I must not be paralysed or moribund but full of life, nurtured by Christ and impelled by his Spirit. I must see others with the eyes of Christ, with all his gentleness and understanding and friendliness. I must listen to others as he listened, with love and patience. Christ wishes to make use of me, of my hands, my capacities, my initiative, in order to help others and to stem evil and distress and ensure the triumph of justice and peace.

Christ wishes to make use of me to go to the poorest of the poor, those who are left destitute and stand in most need of loving care.

Lord, since your life flows in me like the life-stream of blood throughout my body, teach me how to spread awareness of you all around me and let your love shine through in the way I live.

Let my eyes be open wide to the people I meet in daily life. Let my eyes see with your sight.

41

Let my ears be alert to the call of my brothers and sisters.

Let my hands open out to greet and to give. Let them be modelled on yours.

Let my heart be open to those I find difficult to love. Let it be at one with yours.

Teach me so that others may read a welcome in my looks, that my mind may be open to their questioning and to their anxieties. And may I learn to be receptive to your words and your light and the breath of your Spirit.

This image of the Church as the mystical body of Christ is a real treasure; but however appealing it may be we must not neglect other images, otherwise we may run into difficulties. What, for instance, is the relation of people of other religions to the Church; who is and who is not to be considered as a member of Christ; in what sense can those who do not participate integrally in the life of the body be thought of as members?

*   *   *

Father, infinitely good, we give you thanks for all the marvels you have wrought. By our baptism you have united us with the risen Christ and made us, as it were, his members.

Your Church, spread throughout the world, is rightly called the body of Christ, projecting his incarnation amongst all mankind and from century to century.

For 2000 years the Church, stimulated by the Spirit of Christ, has striven to continue its task in the world. Look, Father, upon all those of the past and of today who labour like him to implant his love, his hope and his life wherever they may be.

Look upon us, too, Father, and detect in our lives, our words and our actions traces of the life of Christ, an echo of his words and an extension of his actions. See the whole of humanity, Father, as undergoing the influence of your Spirit. See the efforts made by so many men and women in the cause of greater justice and securely-rooted peace.

See those who, like Christ, give even their lives out of love for others, whatever their race, culture or religion.

Hand-in-hand with them and with all men of good will, with the whole mystical body of the risen Christ, we journey on towards that world which began with his incarnation and that kingdom which will gather together the whole of creation at long last freed from all its ills and from death itself.

Father, your kingdom come!

The Church: temple of God

"God's temple is holy, and that temple you are".
(1 Cor 3,17)

Another term of comparison for the Church which emerges from the New Testament is that of the temple, in other words, any building erected in God's honour; for instance, churches of all styles and sizes in which Christians assemble.

As St Paul went, travelling round on his long missionary journeys, proclaiming Christ everywhere, pagans were converted. They gave up their pagan practices and forsook their idols and their temples so as to become Christians.

Paul told them: Up until now your pagan beliefs led you to build temples to house your idols. From now on you believe in Jesus Christ. Does that mean that you must now build a temple in Christ's honour and in honour of the one true God? Not at all, he told them, the situation is quite different: "The God who made the world and everything in it, being Lord of heaven and earth does not live in shrines made by men" (Acts 17,24). And Paul explained to them that they themselves, each individually and taken all together, are God's temple and as it were living stones with which God builds his house (cf 1 Cor 3).

There is then an enormous difference between the pagan temples of the Greeks and Romans of bygone days and Christian churches.

The pagan temples — you can still see their ruins in Athens and Rome, and around the Mediterranean — were thought of as the dwelling places of the gods. People came there to offer sacrifices and make gifts to obtain favours.

But for us the true dwelling place of God is the living Church of Jesus Christ, the assembly of the Christians. God does not wish to dwell in edifices made with building materials but in the hearts and minds and the very life of men, divinising them, transforming them and making them signs of the new world which is on its way.

We are knit together in one true and unrestricted charity,

God dwells in us and we are truly his temple. When we allow ourselves to be stimulated by the Spirit of Christ, the Spirit of peace, reconciliation and forgiveness, we become the temple of the Holy Spirit. When we pledge ourselves to building up a world of genuine solidarity in which everyone gets his share of food, joy, friendship and freedom, then God dwells in us.

That is the Church we have to build, that Church of living stones cemented together by a single faith and one sole charity. We are living stones sustaining one another's weight and thrust. We stand or fall by the way we hold together. If one of us begins to slip away, those around him are exposed to slipping also. Each has a particular place and function and responsibility to the whole structure. And each must be ready to be worked on and chipped into shape so as to fit exactly in.

This building rests on a single irreplaceable foundation, namely, Jesus Christ. It is in him, says St Paul, that "the whole structure is joined together into a holy temple in the Lord" (Eph 2,21).

It is, indeed, in him that we are fitted together as part and parcel of the whole structure and become a spiritual dwelling place for God.

It is then on Christ that we must build, he who was rejected by the builders of old but is become the corner-stone thanks to which the whole building is held up and forms one harmonious pattern.

The new builders, following St Peter himself — "You are Peter and upon this rock I will build my Church" — are the apostles and prophets and preachers of the Gospel and all who in one way or another proclaim Christ and his message and draw those around them to the faith. They all have to work together in order to further God's task, each according to his abilities. "According to the commission of God given to me", St Paul declares, "like a skilled master builder I laid a foundation, and another man is building upon it. Let each man take care how he builds upon it" (1 Cor 3,10).

This building which is the temple of God must grow until we all attain to the unity of faith and the knowledge of the Son of God, to mature manhood, to the measure of fulness of the stature of Christ (cf Eph 4,13).

It may truly be said that all Christians have responsibility for building up the temple of God. All of us have, after all, to help one another to "build up". Actually the English word "to edify" comes from the Latin word meaning "to build" and is also linked with "edifice". So in edifying our brothers, that is, helping them to build up their Christian lives, we are helping to build up the Church so that one day it will reach its full grandeur and perfection. The perfection of this living edifice where God dwells, the Church, is made up of the perfection achieved by each of its stones, in other words, the holiness and faith and charity of each of the Church's members, those precious stones which catch, as it were, the reflection of the holiness and love of God.

The day when the Church of Christ, the living abode of God, has achieved the fulness of its growth will see the fulfilment of God's plan.

That living dwelling of God, the new humanity, totally transfused by God and alive with his Spirit, is none other than the body of Christ reaching its completeness of growth.

The book of Revelation describes it in terms of the spouse adorned to meet her husband. The risen Christ will make it share his life: "He will wipe away every tear from their eyes, and death shall be no more, neither shall there be mourning nor crying nor pain any more" (Rev 21,4).

It also describes it as the New Jerusalem, the Holy City, shining with the glory of God. It will need the light of neither sun nor moon, for God's glory itself will light it up. And in that City, made up of all the living stones, the elect, there will be no temple because the Lord God will be all in all.

If then, from all we have said, God needs no edifice made of building materials, why do we go on building churches? To answer this we must turn to another meaning of the word church, namely, assembly, albeit it was subsequently used to designate the building where the assembly took place. So our churches are not buildings for God to live in but shelters for Christians to meet in.

So even in this the essential thing is not the building itself but the human beings assembled there. It is they whom God wishes to divinise, share his life with and call to sanctify.

Whilst churches remind us of the presence of God amongst

men, it falls still more to the Christians themselves to be the sign of that presence and to be witnesses of his love by the way they live. While churches are open to all and are places where a single faith and common prayer draw us to meet together despite our many differences as individuals, it is much more our hearts and minds themselves than the mere doors of the church that must be wide open, ever on the lookout for fraternal exchanges, and readily overlooking the quite normal diversities that exist amongst us.

We like our churches to be beautiful buildings, but we should be keener still for the beauty of our faith and charity so as to resemble the seed and the yeast in the parables that speak about the growth of the kingdom of God.

One day, as the crowds stood dazed by the beauty of the Temple in Jerusalem, Jesus declared with sadness in his voice that the day would come when all this splendour will be a ruin with not a stone left upon a stone. Pope John Paul II echoed this when he told the crowds: "All the buildings you look at, St Peter's Basilica, the Vatican and the churches in Rome and in the whole world, a time will come when not a stone of them will rest upon a stone. All will come to ruin". We would find that very sad indeed. And yet, to repeat once more our refrain, it is not the buildings that are essential but the Church itself, the living abode of God built of those living stones which are none other than all the Christians themselves.

That comparison is particularly useful because it provides a quite tangible image of the Church. All the same, we must be on our guard against concluding from it that only those living stones, the baptised, will be counted amongst the elect. When we looked at the Church in terms of the people of God, we were reminded that amongst people who are not Christians all those who believe in God (Jews, Muslims, . . .) are related to the people of God in various ways. "Nor shall divine providence deny those who, without any fault of their own, have not yet arrived at an explicit knowledge of God and who, not without grace, strive to lead a good life" (Lumen Gentium 16).

Perhaps then we might fill out this comparison with the Temple of Jerusalem. At the time of Christ it had an extensive Court of the Gentiles. That shows that even in the Old Testament pagans of good will were already seen to be provided for in God's plan and drawn into its realisation.

There is not the slightest doubt, then, that there are varied degrees of belonging to the Church.

*   *   *

Lord Jesus Christ, you are ever repeating to me, "You too are a living stone in my Church which is being continually built up until the end of time".

There are some stones which play an essential role in keeping the whole building from collapsing, and others that are less important. Lord, help me to see what my place and role are in the Church. Whatever it may be I have responsibility for, other stones adjacent to me. If I am a loose stone or one that is crumbling away, I am no longer supporting others, and I am in danger of sending them tumbling down along with myself.

Some stones are decoratively carved and contribute to making the whole building a thing of impressive beauty. You use this thought, Lord, to remind me that I have my store of responsibility for the beauty and splendour of your living Church. But to ensure this I have to lend myself to being carved by you, and have my egoism, my individualism, my pride chipped away.

Some of the stones seem more sacred than others, like those close in beside the altar and the tabernacle. Others are right out in the open, exposed to the wind and the rain and every passer-by. Lord, maybe I am tempted to reckon myself among the first stones, the closely sheltered ones that everybody stops to admire. But perhaps you really want me to be an outside stone, glared at by the crowds coming and going in the streets and exposed to the weather, getting all the knocks and bumps and scratches.

Lord, whatever happens and wherever I may be placed, I am your Church, your living abode, a sign of your presence amongst men and of your coming kingdom.

Lord, help me always to find my rest in you, the foundation of the whole building, and to ascend towards you, the keystone that keeps the whole structure up. And may I be firmly joined to my brothers by the mortar of faith and love.

The Church: spouse of Christ

"The kingdom of heaven may be compared to a
king who gave a marriage feast for his son...
Everything is ready; come to the marriage feast".
(Mt 22,2.4)

Human dreams are often dreams of love, for men have been created to the image of God and God is love. We should not be surprised therefore to find that God's plan for mankind is a wonder of love.

The story of the created world is the most impressive of all stories of love. Throughout the Bible it is referred to as the "alliance", and not only in the sense of friendship, say, between two tribes or nations, but more specifically between spouses — an alliance of love between God and mankind.

Away back in the Old Testament, in the days, that is, of the ancient alliance — "covenant" and "alliance" are the equivalent of "testament" — the people of Israel, though still a small nation, was already God's beloved and he held out an alliance to them. It comprised, on God's side, a promise of protection and help, guidance, blessing, assured life and peace. Israel, on its side, pledged itself to observe with fidelity the law of God summed up in the Ten Commandments (the Decalogue). "Now therefore", God says, "if you will obey my voice and keep my covenant, you shall be my own possession among all peoples; for all the earth is mine; and you shall be to me a kingdom of priests and a holy nation" (Exod 19,5).

God thus does not start off by describing himself as the Almighty whom everyone must be constrained to acknowledge as Lord and King and to obey subserviently, come what may. Although he is indeed the Lord and does truly possess power over all, God does not wish to wield that power to make us obey out of constraint. Instead he shows himself to his chosen people as one who loves them and calls them to share his life with him and link their destiny with him. God is like a spouse espousing Israel. His people are called to love him with a unique love and he will love them with special love.

49

That then is God as revealed in the Bible.

The word "alliance", therefore, conjures up the union of spouse and espoused, which fits perfectly the relationship God wishes to have towards us. Just as a young man proposes to the lady of his love and hopefully awaits her response, so God in his love for us offers us an alliance with him. He offers to initiate us into his very own life, for his plan — we must never tire of repeating it — is to draw all men to a life of intimate and lasting communion with him and divinise us in teaching us how to love just as he does. And he too awaits our response, taking us as we are and respecting our freedom.

Thus on Mount Sinai, in the days of Moses, was the ancient alliance made, the espousal of God and the people of Israel: "You shalt love the Lord your God with all your heart, and all your soul, and with all your strength" . . . "All the words of the Lord we shall observe".

Just as married couples delight in celebrating the anniversay of their marriage and renewing their marriage vows so also the Bible speaks, time and again, of festivities celebrated to recall and renew the commitment of Israel to its alliance with God.

But despite all this Israel was not always faithful, and the prophets had constantly to raise their voices to admonish them. Through them God represents himself as a spouse who is ever loving even if he has been forgotten, and ever ready to welcome his partner back again if she returns to him. Indeed it is God who takes the initiative: "I will allure her into the wilderness and speak tenderly to her. . . I will betroth you to me in righteousness, and in justice, and in steadfast love, and in mercy. I will betroth you to me in faithfulness; and you shall know the Lord" (Hos 2,14.20).

God does not capitulate in the face of the faithlessness of his people. On the contrary, the prophets bring them his announcement of a new alliance, one which will comprise a change of heart and bring the gift of the Spirit of God: "The days come when I will make a new covenant with you . . . I will give you a new heart and put a new spirit within you. . . I shall put my own spirit in you" (cf Jer 31 and Ezek 36).

The new alliance will be the work of the Servant of Yahweh (the Servant of God) foretold by Isaiah, in whom one finds the traits of the Messiah. "I am the Lord, I have called you in righteousness, I have taken you by the hand, I have given you as a covenant to the people, a light to the nations" (Is 42,6).

While the Old Testament describes God as the spouse who loves his people and calls them to be united with him, the New Testament shows us Christ himself as the spouse who comes to make the new alliance foretold by his prophets.

It is with that in mind that we must read the parables of the marriage feast and the ten virgins: : "The kingdom of God is like a king who made a marriage feast for his son. . ." (cf Mt 22). The king is God, the son is Jesus Christ. As for the bride, she represents the whole of mankind. The great news of the Gospel is that God extends his alliance of love to all men of every nation. He wants to take the whole of humanity as his "bride", to make mankind his very own and share all things with theme.

That indeed is what God has done through Christ by the Incarnation — he has espoused human nature in its entirety, and each and everyone individually. We must not think of the Incarnation as a matter for Christ alone; "for by his Incarnation the Son of God has in a certain way united himself to each man" (Gaudium et Spes 22).

It was on the evening of Holy Thursday, the day before his death, that Christ sealed the new alliance with his apostles. The Last Supper was in a real sense the "wedding feast", the celebration of God's espousal to mankind: "This is my body which will be given up for you. . . This is tthe cup of my blood, the blood of the new and everlasting covenant. It will be shed for you and for all men so that sins may be forgiven".

The terms of the new alliance are no longer simply the terms of the Ten Commandments but a "new commandment" of Christ which far outruns the Decalogue: "A new commandment I give to you, that you love one another; even as I have loved you, that you also love one another. . . Greater love has no man than this, that a man lay down his life for his friends. . . What I have done, do you also for one another" (cf Jn 13 and 15).

On that evening in the Upper Room Jesus had added "Do this in memory of me". In other words, each time you repeat this meal remember that you will be renewing, all together, your commitment and thus ratifying our alliance once more. This is all brought about at Mass.

To share in the Eucharist is to realise in action, for each one of us personally, the new alliance that was enacted on that evening of Holy Thursday and to which each of us became party by our baptism. To celebrate the Eucharist is to celebrate again the espousal of God with mankind and with each single one of us. To receive Communion is to renew our commitment to be faithful to Christ, to love our brothers and sisters as Christ has loved us. It means uniting ourselves all together with Christ so as to be one sole body, heart and mind, with him, just as two spouses accept mutual care for one another, sharing their tasks, their plans, their future and everything. To receive Communion is to open ourselves to the influence of Christ's Spirit of love, coming as he does to transform and divinise us.

It means making God's designs our own and committing ourselves to work ever more thoroughly to help bring about the realisation of his plan for mankind all around us.

It is true that this plan of God for making the whole of mankind his spouse is already achieved radically by the Incarnation but it has still to be made a concrete reality for the mass of mankind. And it does slowly and surely become a reality for all who freely adhere to faith in Jesus Christ and are members of the Church. And of the Church it can be still more emphatically said that it is the spouse of Christ.

St Paul makes that clear in his Letter to the Ephesians. The relationship between husband and wife, he says, must be like the relationship between Christ and his Church. "Husbands, love your wives, as Christ loved the Church and gave himself up for her, that he might sanctify her . . . that he might present the Church to himself in splendour, without spot or wrinkle or any such thing, that she might be holy and without blemish. Even so husbands should love their wives as their own bodies" (Eph 5,25ff).

Christ then has a new, special regard for the Church as his beloved spouse. He wants it to have all splendour and faultlessness, to be holy and irreproachable and responding totally with love for him. He lavishes his care on it, as a spouse does on his beloved.

We know only too well that the Church is far from living up to its proper holiness and good repute. Its robes are often stained and its features blemished. Its shortcomings are so many that they cannot be concealed. Yet Christ loves it still.

St Bernard had this to say on the subject: "The Church is not only the temple of God but also an abode of darkness. It is both a heavenly dwelling and an earthly one, a royal palace and a hovel, a temple of light and a body of death, the spouse of Christ and the butt of the self-elated". But St Bernard goes on to say that the baseness and splendour compensate each other, so that, as each situation arises, good renown redresses the loss of face and saves the Church from being completely crushed by the evils that beset it. And indeed the humiliations play a positive role by heading off the danger of success degenerating into self-complacency. These two factors which seem so incompatible do nevertheless in this way even out, all to the well-being of the bride.

What we must not forget is that each one of us makes up the Church. Its defects and imperfections are always more than likely ours. It is we who, day after day, disfigure it when we are unfaithful to the mind of Christ the spouse, especially with regard to his love and caring for others. Whether the Church maintains, day by day, the beauty and fervour and dynamism of its youth depends on our dedication and energy.

This way of presenting the Church as the bride of Christ has the advantage of emphasising what is of the very essence of Christian living, namely, love.

What is more, love finds its place in every phase of human life and fosters its very being. Love makes the wedded couple what they are supposed to be. Loving care ensures that little ones grow up steadily and become wholesomely aware of the world around them. It is love and solidarity that enable society to be genuinely human. It is love that leads to reconciliation and ensures peace in families and between various groups and nations.

It is through such all-pervading love that God's plan for the world unfolds. Each time I genuinely wish another person well, or with self-forgetfulness give them all my attention and understanding and bring real charity to bear on all around me, there and then I am promoting God's plan — to espouse the whole of humanity, knit together with love.

The book of Revelation foretells the fulfilment of this plan of God at the end of time when, as it were, the seal is set for ever on spouse and bride, in other words, on the union of humanity at long last freed from all its trials. We can hear the voice of the Spirit and the Bride in the words of Revelation:

"Come, Lord Jesus!", that is: Come and take us with you, come and put the final touch to the fulfilment of your work, come and transfigure us and unite us to yourself for ever. And Christ replies: "Surely I am coming soon".

Our faith reaches out with all it has to this eternal future, the everlasting espousal of God with humanity. We firmly believe that God's loving plan will be fulfilled. We firmly believe that out beyond every death there is an outcome, spaciousness and light and love. And that is our own journey's end.

And the day will come when God is all in all.

*   *   *

Lord, you love the Church the way a bride is loved, for all her charm and all her faults or disfigurements. Teach me, then, to love the Church just as it is instead of being critical of it as I am apt to be.

Long ago in Palestine you won over people in their crowds. Why then is it that your Church is so unsuccessful in winning them over today?

You held out a welcome to folk of ill repute, publicans, prostitutes and sinners. Why is it that your Church appears to be so reticent regarding them?

You were close to the lowly folk and understood what they suffered, their joys and the things they set their hearts on. The Church may sometimes appear to be out of touch with them and close to the great folk of society, giving the appearance that it is to them that she is wedded.

You were all eyes and ears for everyone you met. The Church needs to be aware of the daily worries of so many people.

I must confess that I know why it sometimes fails. The short-comings and disfigurements of your Church are all too often quite simply the faults and disfigurements which I contribute. It will depend partly on me whether or not your Church is to show your face to the world, Lord, and be a place of easy dialogue and freedom and peace, where all men feel at home and learn once more to hope.

Lord, most caring Father, give me and give your Church your Spirit of love, the Spirit of Christ himself.

"I am the true vine"

"I am the vine, you are the branches. He who abides in me, and I in him, he it is who bears much fruit".   (John 15,5)

The words "I am the vine, you the branches" give us the last of the comparisons used by Jesus to bring home to us the intimacy of life and love with him to which God calls us as a result of the Incarnation.

The comparison of the body and its members already helped us to grasp it. We saw that after his resurrection and ascension Christ did not leave us, becoming so to speak an extra-terrestrial being. The vine and branches brings out the fact that his incarnation is extended in time. His life on earth has been going on for 2000 years. Far from being limited to the historical setting of his life in the little land of Palestine, his life is spread, one may say, all over the world, wherever Christians are to be found. For it is his life that flows mysteriously in us like the sap of the vine that flows in its branches, and makes them blossom, and nurtures the grapes. It is the same kind of picture as that of the blood flowing through the members of the body and reaching even the tiniest cells in order to nourish them.

Christ is not only "God-with-us" but "God-in-us".

The Church is that enormous vine, rooted in the heart of Christ and growing out all over the globe. Each and every Christian is mysteriously, but really and truly, linked up with Christ.

The branches can only live thanks to the vine. Jesus tells us: "As the branch cannot bear fruit of itself, unless it abides in the vine, neither can you unless you abide in me".

But it is also true that the vine relies on its branches. It is only through them that it produces the grapes.

Thus Christ, living on in his Church, relies on us to be very much alive wherever we live and work. Christ says to each of us: I need you to exercise my influence; I need your heart and your relations with others in order to show my love for those around you; I need your dedication in order to produce fruit.

He counts on us so that he can carry on his work in today's world, his task of drawing people together in one fraternal gathering in justice and in love. Once we have thoroughly grasped that, our outlook is changed. When we meet cases of suffering, want or violence, instead of hollow lamentations about "how could God let such things happen" we ought to ask ourselves how we Christians and human beings can have let them happen when God is counting on us to see that they do not.

When we see suffering or moral or physical wretchedness we should listen to God who is calling us as Moses was once called: "I have seen the affliction of my people. . . I know their sufferings and I have come to deliver them. . . Come, I will send you . . . that you may bring forth my people. . . I will be with you" (cf Exod 3).

You note that it is together and at one-and-the-same-time that God and Moses are to deliver the people; God in and through Moses. God will do nothing without him and Moses will do nothing except with God. And so it is with us today. We are the branches of Christ, he does nothing without us and whatever we do we are to do only with him.

Clearly then, as we have said, the life of Christ is not confined to his lifetime spent in Palestine but comprises also his life since the Resurrection, the life he now lives through his vine, that is, the Church, the thousands of millions of Christians.

It is we who have to ensure that he is seen to be truly alive in the world of today. We, indeed, as we have said, are his branches, his members, his extended presence amongst men. We must not let Christ die within us, for that would spell the death of the world.

In the allegory of the vine the expression "bear fruit" is repeated again and again. What is this fruit we must constantly bear?

The Gospel is not slow in telling us: "This is my commandment that you love one another as I have loved you. . . This I command you, to love one another".

Once more, then, Christ insists: we must live as he does with love for others so that his Church may be, as it were, a glimpse of the shape of God's kingdom.

There are two aspects of this commandment of love. There is the universal aspect: God is love, and his love extends to all —

he causes the sun to rise and the rain to fall on the good and the bad, on the honest and the dishonest, on Christians and non-Christians. Love impels us to treat all men as our brothers and to commit ourselves to building a truly new world where all can have their share of life and friendship.

Besides this there is the ecclesial aspect of love. Some Christians seem unaware of it. The fact that Christ wishes us to practise a universal love does not mean that we should neglect those closest to us and in particular our Christian brethren themselves.

When Christ told his apostles to love one another, he certainly did not neglect this first aspect of Christian love. It is easy enough to love the little Chinese children who live so far away. But what is keeping us from loving our neighbour who comes to Mass every Sunday and to welcome those to whom we have never so far said "good day"? And what keeps us from loving that other neighbour who never goes to Mass but whom we pass almost daily in the street?

The Church, we said, must be a glimpse of the shape of the kingdom of God. In the Church, then, it must be possible to discern the way one is to behave in that new world of God's eternal plan for mankind. How can the Church claim to be behaving that way when Christians, who come together for the Holy Eucharist, give no evidence of affection for one another but only perform those vague gestures of politeness one shows to just anyone one happens to run into in the grocer's shop or on the train? To talk of Christian communities where there is no love just does not make sense. And they can bear no fruit. Set amongst the divisions and clashes of our world they cannot possibly be seen as places of reconciliation, hope and friendship.

We must at all costs build up Christian commuities made up of all kinds of people in which, as in the time of Christ, all are welcome and in which kindliness is extended to the publican and pharisee, the leper and the prostitute, the revolutionary and the traditionalist.

The kind of Christian communities that attract people are those open to all, places that are friendly and warm-hearted, with Christians happy to meet one another, Churches that are not purely dogmatic but also friendly and fraternal. "See how they love one another", is what people said about the first Christians. Such communities are sign of the kingdom of God.

They are a foretaste of the world God planned for mankind. In the vine it is they that are the branches that produce the fruit. They contribute to the glory and the joy of God. "By this is my Father glorified", said Jesus (Jn 15,8).

To achieve all this, Christ sets out three conditions.

First, we must be thoroughly united with him as the branches are with the vine. "Abide in me as I abide in you. . . He who abides in me and I in him, he it is who bears fruit in abundance".

This word "abide" recurs again and again in chapter 15 of St John's gospel. It conveys something more than mere physical closeness or neighbourhood. It suggests rather a real friendship and intimacy. It means being at home with someone and sharing, as husband and wife do in a household.

The key to all this is love. First the love of God: "If anyone loves me my Father will love him". Second, love as such: "God is love, and he who abides in love abides in God, and God abides in him" (1 Jn 4,16).

The second condition is that we must gladly allow ourselves to be pruned and purified: "Every branch that bears fruit he prunes that it may bear more fruit".

This is self-evident. You cannot commit yourself to loving unless you are ready to give up your personal preferences for the sake of the people you love. Love is always a gift of self, as St Paul told the Christians of Corinth (cf 1 Cor 13). Love means patience, service to others, self-forgetfulness, self-control, kindliness, forgiveness, openness to others. This is not always an easy task. It means hacking away at our own pride and our egoism and resentment, and sometimes even our personal tastes and legitimate freedom. St Paul said he was free to eat any kind of meat he liked, but that if in doing so he ran the risk of scandalising one of his brethren he would give up eating such and such a type of meat rather than be the cause of unsteadying his brother. And Jesus tells us that such considerations can even entail total self-sacrifice: "Greater love has no man than this, that he lay down his life for his friends".

The third condition is that we must be nurtured on Christ as the branches are nourished by the sap from the vine.

We must draw nourishment from his teaching and his example: "If you abide in me and my words abide in you, ask whatever you will and it shall be done to you".

And we must draw nourishment from the living presence of Christ in the Eucharist: "As the living Father sent me, and I live because of the Father, so he who eats me will live because of me" (Jn 6,57).

God's desire is that his vine should grow and spread more and more so that signs of the new world, the kingdom of God, make their appearance everywhere.

And when the vine spreads it is the risen Christ himself who reaches out "until we attain to the unity of the faith . . . to the mature manhood, to the measure of the stature of the fulness of Christ" (Eph 4,13).

When that comes about it will be both the perfect fulfilment of God's plan and the perfect fulfilment of humanity.

We firmly believe that this ultimate fulfilment will one day come. Indeed, Christians are not alone in striving for that end. People of other religions do so, and even non-believers. There are so many striving to improve the world, so many bodies pledged to helping the underprivileged, so much unseen dedication and sacrifice that brings a touch of joy and love into lives where joy and love are unknown.

Later on we shall have something to say about the mysterious way the Spirit of Christ is wafted everywhere, and in the least expected places shoots imperceptibly sprout from the vine which is Jesus Christ.

*   *   *

Lord God, how wonderful you are that you should love us thus. In times gone by you made your people your chosen vine, and lavished your love and care on it. You expected it to produce fine grapes, and all it did was to give worthless fruit.

And so you sent us your Son, Jesus Christ. He himself is the true vine, and we are his branches nurtured by his own life and his Spirit.

Indeed, Lord, how wonderful you are to love us so.

And what of you, Jesus Christ, that you should love us so? You are not only God-with-us but God-in-us. You come to dwell in us and we dwell in you in a closeness we would never have dreamt of. You take possession of us by your Spirit to teach us to love others as ourselves. How wonderful you are that you should love us so.

And what of you, Spirit of God, that you should love us? You are the breath that sets us all alive, the power which energises us, the light by which we see. You are the flowing stream watering everything with life. You are the fire of which Christ said, "I came to cast fire on the earth, and would that it were already kindled so that all mankind might be aflame with it".

Spirit of God, how wonderful you are that you should love us so.

The Holy Spirit beyond-the-boundaries

*"In the last days it shall be, God declares, that I
will pour out my Spirit upon all flesh. Being
therefore exalted at the right hand of God, and
having received from the Father the promise of the
Holy Spirit, he has poured out this which you see
and hear".* (Acts 2,17.33)

The Holy Spirit inspires and stimulates the Church and all
Christians. He urges them to live in union with the risen Christ
and united to one another in love, like members that belong
to one single body or the bride made one with her husband or
the branches joined inseparably to the vine.

But the Holy Spirit is also at work beyond the boundaries of
the Church. Away back in the Old Testament we read: "The
Spirit of God fills the whole world". And Christ in his turn
said: "The Spirit is like a wind that blows where it will". Why
then should he claim to confine it within the boundaries of the
Church? Surely we are not envious of all that he does for those
outside and the light to which he opens their eyes.

It has been said that the name "Holy Spirit" is God's
missionary title. On the first Pentecost day he impelled the
apostles from the Upper Room where they had shut themselves
up for fear of the Jews. You do not imagine that he intended
to let himself be locked up there himself! Quite the contrary,
ever since that day, the "Spirit of God has been poured out on
all flesh" (Acts 2,17).

For the Holy Spirit, then, there is no such thing as a foreign
land. He is at home everywhere. He is present in the heart
of every person of whatever race, tongue, culture or
religion.

The Second Vatican Council, in its Constittuion on the Church
in the Modern World, says: "Since Christ died for all and since
all men are in fact called to the same destiny, which is divine,
we must hold that the Holy Spirit offers to all the possibility
of being made partners, in a way known to God, in the paschal
mystery" (Gaudium et Spes 22).

The sower scatters the seed everywhere, on the paths, the

61

stoney ground, amongst the thorns and also on good soil. So also the Holy Spirit sows his gifts and his light on all men wherever they may be. With the future harvest in mind he endeavours to make the seeds germinate everywhere. In every germ of goodness in the hearts and thoughts of men, in their cultures, customs or religions, we can detect the invisible work of the Holy Spirit.

What is implied when we speak of the Holy Spirit "endeavouring", "working",' "acting", in regard to non-Christians? It means first of all that the Holy Spirit is preparing their hearts to willingly accept Christ's message at such time as Christians or missionaries come to bring it to them.

When therefore we approach somebody, even one to all appearances remote from the one true God, we believe that the Holy Spirit has been operating there before we ever started. Whether it is youngsters, fiancés soon to be married, fellow-workers of our own nationality or from abroad, or just someone in our neighbourhood, we know that in each of them there are hidden treasures and concealed aspirations which are the fruit of the seeds planted there by the Holy Spirit. For he has always gone before us, entering the minds and hearts of people, opening them up, making them ready and willing to accept the light when it is brought.

The Acts of the Apostles tell how the apostle Peter was led to meet the centurion Cornelius and his family. The Holy Spirit had made everything ready and "the believers who came with Peter were amazed, because the gift of the Holy Spirit had been poured out even on the Gentiles" (Acts 10,45).

Later on it will be Paul's turn to experience the same thing. At the time when the Gospel had not yet been brought to Macedonia. Paul, at Troas, had a vision in which he saw a man from Macedonia who begged him to "come over and help us". Paul took a ship and went to Philippi, the principal town in the region, took part in a prayer meeting and spoke about Christ.

The Acts of the Apostles records that a woman named Lydia was there, and that "the Lord opened her heart to give heed to what was said by Paul". She was baptised with her whole household (cf Acts 16,14).

A little later on, at Corinth, the Lord alerted Paul: "Do not be afraid, but speak . . . I am with you . . . for I have many people in this city" (Acts 18,9). Clearly the Holy Spirit had been at work. We find the same idea developed in St John's gospel when Christ says: "No one can come to me unless the Father who sent me draws him. . . It is written in the prophets, 'And they shall all be taught by God' " (Jn 6,44–45). So it is that the Father, through the work of the Holy Spirit, has constantly drawn to Christ men and women of good will prepared to receive the Gospel message wholeheartedly the moment it is made known to them.

It might all be summed up like this. Beyond the boundaries of the already existing Church membership you can detect clear, even if rudimentary, traces of the presence of the Spirit of God at work within all kinds of human efforts at finding solutions and fraying a path, however unpromising, towards attaining justice, peace and brotherly concern, all coupled with self-sacrificing dedication to fostering these universal values.

The wide-awake Christian feels quite at home in all this and realises that the Church and these people of good will are speaking much the same language.

After all, it is surely the voice of the Spirit that speaks through both. The masterhand of the Spirit is everywhere at work ahead of us. It is sometimes said that it is the void left by the lack of God's presence that calls us to go to our unbelieving brothers. Rather it is the presence of the Spirit of God in their midst that draws us towards them. We go to them because God, who is already there, invites us to be their companions, to be witnesses of his presence, and open their eyes to it.

Thus the Spirit is the first missionary, and the world at large is not to be thought of as a spiritual desert. God did not wait for our intervention to love mankind and take action for their sake!

Many a priest and many a Christian have time and again become aware of this presence of God in the hearts of people who have no contact whatsoever with the visible Church. To quote just one case. There was a woman who had been brought up from childhood in a state orphanage where no religious education of any kind is given. She married at the age of sixteen, left her husband after eighteen months, and so drifted on. Yet, at the age of sixty-five, despite her total lack of religious knowledge, she prayed every day, cared lovingly for her invalid mother-in-law and had a real hunger and thirst for God. The Lord is almost a totally unknown person to her, and yet she is by no means an unknown person to him for he loves her and is at work within her.

The Spirit of God likewise breathes and is at work in the hearts of people in the places where the Church falls short of what it ought to be, or is seen simply as an ecclesiastical religious administrative machine, or where Christians do anything but give a true picture of what a Christian should be.

The parable of the tenants of the vineyard (cf Mt 21) makes exactly that point. True, in the time of Christ it was geared directly to the behaviour of the Jewish religious authorities, but it is easily applicable to the Church. The tenants who neglect the vine can be seen as representing authorities of the Church in some place or other, no longer bearing proper witness to Christ and his message. The Church, taken as one whole body, has been given the guarantee of indefectibility by Christ himself. But that does not necessarily apply to the Church in every particular spot. The Church in a given place, in such or such diocese or country might find itself hearing the Lord say to it: "The kingdom of God will be taken away from you".

In other words, Christ forewarns us that we, the Christians in such and such a place, are his visible Church and the chief means he wishes to use to bring the people his message of truth, love and peace, and that if we are not faithful to that mission, and if our Christian community fails to be seen as the seed of his kingdom, his Spirit will turn to others, regardless of their religious or philosophical notions. For it is quite true that "the kingdom of God will be taken away from you and given to a people producing the fruits of it".

The parable of the banquet and the ill-mannered guests (cf Lk 14) carries the same lesson. If the members of the Church turn a deaf ear to the Lord and put their own personal preoccupations before concern for his kingdom, he will call to himself the poor and the maimed and the blind and the lame, all those who would never have dreamt that anyone would think of them, and send them an invitation.

Above all, the Spirit of God breathes and is at work in places, cultures and civilisations where the Church has so far been unable to penetrate and take root. For there, as everywhere else, there are men and women of good will, and the Holy Spirit is at work in the hearts and the lives of all of them.

"At work" here, as always, means that the Holy Spirit is the Spirit of love of the Father and the Son, and whenever he breathes it is always in order to impel people to love, and to do so ever better and more generously. "The fruit of the Spirit", St Paul tells us, "is love, joy, peace, patience, kindness, goodness, faithfulness, gentleness, self-control" (Gal 5,22).

You notice that the "fruit" (in the singular) of the Spirit is love. The list Paul goes on to give consists of the signs of the presence of the kingdom of love, namely, joy and peace. Then come the ways this love is shown, namely, patience, kindness, goodness. And lastly there are the conditions for the growth of love: faithfulness, gentleness and self-control.

Once again, then, the fruit of the Spirit is love. It is by this that we are linked with God, for God himself is love. It is then love which divinises us and makes us like to God. You might say that love is, as it were, the first sacrament.

Jesus himself alludes to this in the parable of the Last Judgment (cf Mt 25). We see a gathering of people of all the nations on earth, all races, cultures, religions. The Lord does not ask them whether they are Christians, Buddhists, Muslims, Jews, or Hindus, or whether they have practised penance, prayed and fasted. What he asks is whether they shared what they had with others — given food to the hungry, cared for the sick, have welcomed the stranger, visited the imprisoned. In a word, he asks whether they have shown love for others. And he adds tellingly: What you did for them you did to me. Everything done for others unites you with me. Your acts of love for others are a sign that you are ramifications of me, like the branches and the vine, and a sign that you are alive with my life by which you are divinised.

The same teaching is given in the parable of the Good Samaritan. By statute the Samaritans were separate from the Jewish people of God. And yet the Lord held this Samaritan up as an example of what love of others and love of God should be. And what precisely had the Samaritan done to merit that? He had come to the help of a total stranger lying by the roadside.

We can then speak of love as the first sacrament in this sense, that sacraments are outward signs which establish a relationship between us and God and divinise us. The practice of love is a sign that we are willingly stimulated by the Spirit of God, and "all who are led by the Spirit of God are sons of God" (Rom 8, 14).

It is true, therefore, to say that the Holy Spirit suscitates in the visible Church an invisible reaching-out beyond itself, in spiritual matters that know no bounds, a reaching-out to every type of milieu, race and religion. The Holy Spirit finds disciples everywhere. Many of them may never come to know the person of Christ, yet the Holy Spirit strikes a chord deep in their consciences which sets a distinctive seal on their daily lives and in their relations with other people. They are in circumstances in which baptism will never come their way, but the love which pervades their hearts and stimulates them links them without a doubt to Christ and to God who is love.

So it is that the Holy Spirit raises up men and women by means of whom the kingdom of God is extended and God's plan is quietly and unobtrusively carried forward — that drawing of mankind together in Christ and in love so that God may be all in all.

How wonderful will be our surprise when we come to see this immense crowd, which no man can number, of every tribe and tongue and people and nation.

What joy it is to realise that the Spirit of God is so free and so unfettered. We must see to it that our souls know no bounds and that our hearts are open to all, since the kingdom of God knows no bounds and the heart of God is open to all.

*   *   *

Lord, I know that for you there is no such thing as a foreign land or race or religion. For the presence of your Spirit fills the whole world and you are at work even in the hearts of those we might be tempted to think of as most hostile and uninterested.

It is all too true that everywhere, as indeed in ourselves, there are weeds entangled with the good seed. But I know that you are to be found wherever people aspire to greater justice and brotherliness, or wherever they seek the light of truth, or strive for a better world in which love and peace can flourish. When the desire for mutual understanding eliminates war, or forgiveness surmounts a thirst for vengeance and love triumphs over hatred, we owe it all to you.

Teach me, Lord, to detect the signs of your presence in the people I shall meet today. Teach me to behave towards them exactly as you would do. Teach me to speak to them, not to draw attention to myself, but in a way that will make your presence felt and your hidden word spring to life.

Truly the day of harvesting will eventually come. Then, Lord, your plan for mankind will be realised and all men down the ages will together share in your life and your love.

The Eucharist

"Do this in remembrance of me".

(Luke 22,19)

The Holy Spirit, as we have seen, works at the heart of men and women and in the world at large. Surely then he must be at work in the heart of the Church and of Christians. He does this specially through the sacraments, and among the sacraments the Eucharist expresses best of all the effect of the Holy Spirit's action through the threefold transformation this sacrament produces.

First there is the change in the bread and wine. Bread and wine are full of meaning. They stand for the entire life of man, all his labour and all the struggles he has in order to ensure a normal existence. The bread comes from the work of the farmer and the trader. Workmen, artisans, researchers, various employees and mothers at home, all play a part. And we can think of it, too, as representing professional, social and family life. In a word the bread represents the whole of mankind.

At the moment of the consecration Christ, in a mysterious way, makes all that his own body by the power of the Spirit. The consecration of the bread and wine at Mass is, as it were, a seed from which can grow the transformation of the whole of the creation.

In God's plan the whole of man's life and work are meant to be divinised in Christ. St Paul tells us that "the whole of creation has been groaning in travail" awaiting its liberation and transformation" (cf Rom 8).

But it is up to us to undertake a preliminary cleansing of human life and activity from their all-too-common blemishes — hard-heartedness, oppressiveness, injustice, violence. . . For none of this can enter the kingdom of God.

The consecration at Mass, then, reminds us that the whole world has to be transformed, recapitulated in Christ and gathered together under one head, namely, Christ.

The second transformation is that the risen Christ gradually transforms us into himself by the power of the Spirit, nourishing us with his own living person.

Unlike ordinary food, which is transformed into ourselves, the purpose of this spiritual food of the Eucharist, which is the risen Christ, is to transform us into his own body and make us alive with his life.

In the third transformation, the risen Christ, by offering us all a share of the consecrated bread, gathers us and binds us together, we who are so easily scattered and divided in our ordinary round of life.

This transformation of the Church, which is all too often disjointed, makes it one body in which all is communion and fraternal sharing. This is accurately expressed in all the Eucharistic Prayers. Thus: "May all of us who share in the body and blood of Christ be brought together in unity by the Holy Spirit" and "Grant that we may become one body, one spirit in Christ".

How can we receive Communion without realising the demand made on us to strive for all we are worth at sharing and brotherliness?

Thus the wording of the prayers of the Mass speaks clearly of the work of the Holy Spirit. He is the central figure at work renewing all things, unifying, divinising, in order to foster the growth of the risen body of Christ until it reaches the "fulness of its stature".

The following reflections will bear this out.

PREPARATION OF THE GIFTS

Blessed are you, Lord, God of all creation, through your goodness we have this bread (this wine) to offer which earth has given and human hands have made. It will become for us the bread of life (our spiritual drink).

For bread and wine read everything that makes up our lives as men and women, our work, our home life, friendships, encounters, joys, struggles and sufferings. We include, too, the structures of society, local, national, international. We include the whole of creation, all this material world.

We owe it all to you, Lord: our very being, our surroundings, our social and home setting, our country, the whole universe. You gave it all to us for us to improve it and make it more human, and in our turn we give it back to you so that you may mark it with your divinity.

Yes, Lord, with this bread and wine it is the whole of mankind that we offer you, the whole universe awaiting its liberation. We offer it so that it may be transformed and renewed and gathered in the risen Christ.

PREFACE

Father, we give you thanks for your plan for spreading love upon the earth.

Before the foundation of the world you chose us in Christ that we should be holy and blameless before him. You destined us in love to be your sons through Jesus Christ, according to the purpose of your loving will, to the praise of your glory.

It is through Christ that all things were created. He is before all things and in him all things have their end. It is he whom you foresaw before ever the world was made.

In him and through him, through his incarnation, death and resurrection, you have wished to cure all things, pardon and reconcile, transform and divinise all things, and sum up all things, so that all things might be filled with his fulness, and that in him we might come to the fulness of life and love.

We give you thanks, Father, for everything that fosters the fulfilment of your plan for the world: the countless tokens of love and caring performed every day in mankind; the myriad acts of solidarity and humble service to others sparked off by your Spirit in the secret of the hearts of men and women, which are known to you alone; all the lives consecrated and spent for the service of others.

Deep in all such acts and lives we recognise, Father, the work of your Spirit, the risen Christ growing ever more widely. And we recognise you as the One who comes to fill all creation with your glory and your love.

Holy, holy, holy Lord, God...

EUCHARISTIC PRAYER

Lord, you are holy indeed, the fountain of all holiness. Let your Spirit come upon these gifts to make them holy; let this bread and wine be transformed and become the real sign of the living presence of Christ; let our minds and thoughts be pervaded by your Spirit and your thoughts; let us become ever better members of your body; let our society and all nations become aware of your message of love and reshape themselves by making that message their rule of life; let the world and the entire universe one day become the body of Christ.

Take and eat, this is my body which will be given up for you.

Take and drink, this is my blood. It will be shed for you.

Do this in memory of me.

Take and eat.

Nourish yourselves on me. Nourish yourselves on my living presence, my thoughts, my words, my mind, my love, as I nourish myself on the life of my Father, on his love, his will. For my food is to do the will of my Father.

This is my body which will be given up for you. I give myself to you, to each and everyone, as I gave myself in one single act to the whole of humanity at the moment of my incarnation. Remain in me and I in you, as I am in the Father and the Father in me.

Take and drink.

My blood, that is, my life. My blood shed for you means my life given drop by drop out of love for you and for the mass of mankind. Let my life and my love pervade you and stimulate you, flow in all of you — you who are my members, the branches of the vine — so that little by little they will transform you.

Do this in memory of me.

"Do this" means: let all of you together renew this meal which will transform you and gather you all to me in unity. "Do this" means: give your life for others, in imitation of me and with me. Your celebration of the Eucharist must not be thought of as only a reminder of my sacrifice of 2000 years ago, a reminder of my passage from death to life. It is the celebration of my Pasch actually within yourselves, you coming with me to a life animated ever more and more by my Spirit of love.

Every time the Eucharist is offered it celebrates the Pasch of the whole Church constantly carrying out its mission. Each time, it foretells the Pasch of the great family of mankind, namely, the day when creation will at last be set free from sin and death.

Lord, in enacting here the memorial of the death and resurrection of Christ, we offer you, through the consecrated bread and wine, the whole life of Christ, placed at the service of your plan, that life of Christ absorbed in love of you, Father, and love of his human brothers. In his life you found all your joy, for in him was realised to perfection the ideal man you had always envisaged in your plan for mankind.

We give you thanks because you have chosen us in him and for him to serve and pursue his task.

We humbly beg that while we share the body and blood of Christ we may be brought together by the Holy Spirit as members of one body. And we pray that Christ's work for the gathering together of all his scattered children may constantly progress.

Look, Lord, on your Church, spread throughout the world. May it be an ever more faithful sign of your kingdom, a true reflection of the face of Christ, a centre of truth and freedom, the home of love, justice and peace, where every single person may find both light and hope.

Look, Lord, on the whole human race with your Spirit at work within it. Look on all those men and women of good will who, despite their shortcomings, sincerely wish the world to be a more fraternal place and who strive to make it so.

Lord, look on this human race going on its way. Urged on by your Spirit, through all its ups and downs, it goes forward towards your kingdom which at long last will assemble in Jesus Christ — a transfigured universe.

Through him, with him, in him . . . the whole Christ journeying towards his plenitude, in the Holy Spirit who binds us and all things in unity, all our love and thanksgiving and all honour and glory be yours, Father, for ever.

OUR FATHER

Father, to whom we owe our existence.

Father, who called us to be your children by baptism.

Father, who sends us the Holy Spirit to teach us how to conduct our lives according to your ways, your preferences, your mind.

Father, whose great desire is to see in us the reflection of the face of Christ your beloved Son, since you created us in his image and likeness.

Our Father who art in heaven. . . You who are everywhere in the universe and to spread around it reflections of your beauty.

Hallowed by thy name. . . Make yourself known as God through the action of your Spirit as the history of mankind unfolds, through the life, death and resurrection of Christ, through your Church and its saints, men and women of good will who seek you, even those who are drawn to you although they do not know you yet. Make yourself known as the God of love and pardon to everyone we meet today.

Thy kingdom come. . . Your kingdom of love, justice and peace. Your reign over mankind steadily advancing towards one great fraternal body. Your kingdom which will transform the universe into a totally new world, a new creation. Your kingdom in which you will be all in all.

Thy will be done on earth as it is in heaven. . . It is your will that not one of these least ones be lost; that all men may have life and have it fully; that your disciples may love one another as Christ loved us; that all mankind may become the body of your Son; that we all remain attached to him as the branch is to the vine; that we dwell in him as he dwells in us; that we produce fruit, fruit that will last. It is your will that the Church may love you and be to Christ a faithful spouse; that the day of everlasting espousals may come soon, the day when all things will be summed up and divinised in your Son.

Give us this day our daily bread. . . The bread we need to keep physically alive, all we need in order to grow and be fulfilled materially; the bread which so many of our fellowmen are tragically deprived of because we have yet to learn what sharing really means; the bread our hearts hunger for: friendship, people who love us and people we can love; the bread our minds need: truth and things of beauty; the bread our soul and our life need: the living bread, Christ Jesus who comes to shape us all to his likeness.

Forgive us our trespasses as we forgive those who trespass against us. . . Forgive us, cure us, set us once more on the true way. Do not leave us behind but come and seek your lost sheep. Welcome home your child, restore his life and his happiness. Reconcile us with yourself and amongst ourselves, so that your members are restored to the unity and your children are gathered together once more in mutual love; so that your people, freed from their fetters, may once more journey on towards you.

Lead us not into temptation. . . It is by enduring trials that we grow; but let not the trials be so overwhelming that we succumb.

73

But deliver us from all evil . . . from mediocrity; from all that makes for division and estrangement; from all that keeps us far from you; from all that halts us as we move towards you; from all resentment, fear and doubt; from all that can blind us; from all that makes us deaf to your call and the call of our fellowmen; from all illusions; from the pursuit of false riches; from the meshes of attachment to transient things that prevent us from going forward to things of ultimate value.

COMMUNION

This is the Lamb of God, the Lord Jesus Christ, who comes to be our guide, our companion on our way, our friend who both makes himself at home with us and invites us to stay with him.

Communion is sharing the bread and wine; sharing of hearts and happiness and love, of our most secret thoughts and desires. Communion is treasures of Christ given spontaneously to man, and man in his penury giving himself to Christ.

It is communion with Jesus Christ who is life, love and light; with Christ who heals and nourishes and transforms. It is the wedding feast, the espousals of God and humanity in the risen Christ. It spells joy of man and joy of God.

Lord, nourish us with your words, your Spirit, your forgiveness, your body, your life.

Lord, transform us, so that we may all be truly one and truly one with you.

Go in peace. . . Go into the whole world and preach the Gospel to all creation. I am with you always; yes, to the end of time.

Praying during Advent

A time of expectation

*"Awaiting our blessed hope, the appearing of the
glory of our great God and Saviour Jesus Christ".*
(Tit 2,13)

Looking forward is so typical of human life.

The youngster just cannot wait for the holidays to come.

The expectant mother is all wrapped up in the coming birth
of her child.

The farmer is for ever watching his prospective harvest.

Oppressed peoples yearn for their freedom.

The starving hunger and thirst for food.

The sick anxiously look forward to being well again.

The young man can think only of meeting his fiancée.

Everyone's mind and heart is set on something to come, the
return of spring, living one's life, love, bright new days of
happiness. And awaiting spells active involvement: the expectant mother, the evolving universe, a striving humanity.

And God himself is ever at work: he too abides the fulfilment
of his plans, desiring their realisation, biding his time patiently
from the days of Adam and Eve, Abraham and Moses, the
Prophets, Israel in exile...

He waited until his people were ready to respond. He waited
for the reply of the humble Virgin. He waited for the response
of all those who looked forward in hope.

Advent looks forward with a twofold expectation and hope:
man's expectation and God's.

It recalls the scene at Jacob's well: Christ consciously awaited
the Samaritan woman; she lived in expectation of the coming
of the Messiah.

It is only in the dead and inanimate things that one finds no
trace of expectation.

Happy are those who await in hope for the eternal holiday
of heaven, the birth of a new heaven and earth, the harvest

home of the kingdom of God, the security of final freedom, the spring of Living Water for eternal life.

Whoever drinks of this water will never thirst again. It brings healing for every wound and every ill.

And God will wipe away every tear from their eyes.

Why Lord do you wait?

"With the Lord one day is as a thousand years, and a thousand years as one day. The Lord is not slow about his promise as some count slowness, but is forbearing towards you". (2 Pet 3,8–9)

Why, Lord, do you wait to intervene? See what a state we are in! All those innocent people tortured and imprisoned, the catastrophes that sweep people wholesale to their death, the violence and the wars that go on and on. Lord, can you really be unconscious of it all? Arise, then, Lord and come to our help. Why, Lord, do you wait to intervene?

But, on reflection, how can we place all these troubles at your door when we ought to be taking ourselves to task, each one of us? You entrusted the universe to us, meaning us gradually to master it and share out its riches amongst ourselves and place creation at the service of the whole of mankind.

Instead inertia, lack of concern, egotism, thirst for domination have taken over at the cost of loving concern for others and a spirit of sharing. It is we, Lord, who are blocking the growth of your kingdom. You would have us baptised in the Holy Spirit, as John the Baptist put it, and steep us and the world in your Spirit of love and brotherliness. But we must first needs be plunged by you into cleansing waters so as to be converted and have our hearts changed.

Lord, how wonderful your patience is! You are not one to blast your way through the barriers we have set up. You leave us free to behave as we wish, even in our wilful misdeeds.

It is left to me, to all of us, to remove the obstacles that lay in your path so that your hopes for us may be fulfilled.

How all-embracing your hopes are! You would have no child left destitute, no old-aged person left uncared for, the suffering welcomed with compassion. You would have the poorest of the poor find themselves as well thought of as the well-to-do, immigrants made to feel at home and treated kindly, the people of the Third World properly fed, the unemployed not to be written off but able to lead a meaningful life, my neighbour in distress knowing he can come and tell me his troubles and find in me a friend.

Well may I ask myself, Lord, why I am holding back?

Lives that speak for themselves

"They said to him then, 'Who are you? ... What do you say about yourself?' He said, 'I am the voice of one crying in the wilderness. Make straight the way of the Lord' ". (Jn 1,22–23)

When the officials came from Jerusalem to query John the Baptist's identity he told them that he was the voice crying in the wilderness, "Make straight the way of the Lord". That was exactly his mission, the task set him. He was passionately absorbed in it and identified with it. "No, I am not the Messiah. You must not attach yourselves to me but to Christ. It is he you must love and follow. It is he who is the light. As for me, I am just preparing the way for him".

Such is John the Baptist's message. Everything about him speaks of Christ and proclaims his coming. "I am a voice calling to people, crying out to alert them. Apart from that, what is there to say for myself. You have only to look at the way I live and behave day in, day out. It speaks for itself — a life that cries out the name of Christ, a ceaseless song of his praise".

When two young people are in love they do not need to put it into words. You have only to look at them to see it even when they do not realise how evident it is.

A Christian is someone wrapped up in the love of Christ. That too ought to show through. His whole life ought to sing of Christ and speak out his message.

When Christ told his apostles that he did not call them servants but friends, he was surely thinking of us all — of me, too.

And am I shy, Lord, of being known as your friend? It is you yourself who urge me constantly on, deep down within myself. Day after day, through me and in me, you wish to go on bringing the good news to the poor, to stand by those who are spurned or never given a thought, to heal the broken hearted, to announce deliverance to the imprisoned of all kinds, and freedom to those in captivity. May everything about me, Lord, sing of you and cry out your love to all who seek your face.

Come, Lord Jesus!

"Come, Lord Jesus! . . . Surely, I am coming".
(Rev 22,20)

This morning around 8 o'clock, I was in the Underground packed with people. Lots of them looked half-asleep, going off to their day's work with no particular sign of delight! The routine commuters.

Just seeing them sitting there each keeping himself to himself, I could not help wondering what they were all thinking about. What did life mean to them? Were they aware that God loved them and called them to share his love, that they are journeying towards a New World, God's world, where the be all and end all is spelt out with love?

And yet they all most probably had some love in their lives, like someone they are engaged to, or a wife, parents, children, friends. They all surely feel that need to love and be loved which marks us off as somebody and gives our life a motive.

And that, after all, is the trace of God in our lives: the opening up of our lives to the source of love, to God himself who secretly beckons us on.

But who will make all these people in the tube aware of that presence of God surrounding them with his love, and aware that God is indeed beckoning to them to open their hearts to him and to their fellowmen?

And who will make them realise that the joy we experience in loving here and now is but a prelude to the joy to come, a fulness of love and a quite other joy to which we have all been called?

* * *

Lord Jesus Christ, you have let me know your secret. . . You count on me, on all of us, to make it known to others. . . You are a God of tenderness, the source of all life and love, ever close to everyone whoever they may be. Our heart is ever restless until it rests in you, for you have made us for yourself.

Teach me, Lord, to proclaim the good news, not only by word of mouth but, like you, by acts of sharing and love and solidarity, showing love for others, rekindling their hope and courage, putting them on the right path. May your Church be a place where people feel at home and experience love, a place where everyone can clearly see in your light the ultimate meaning of life.

Come, Lord Jesus!

Mary of Nazareth

"He who is mighty has done great things for me".
(Lk 1,49)

Lord, with Mary of Nazareth I sing in your praise, "He who is mighty has done great things for me".

Why was it, Lord, that you chose her from amongst the thousands of young women in your people? It was simply because she was one of those least ones in the world of that time: humble, sincere believers, the poor at heart, the kind in whom you always find delight. It is by the secrets of the heart that you judge and not by mere externals.

The young Mary of Nazareth was not in the habit of admiring her own qualities, reckoning up her merits. She was not one of those proud people with hearts set on wealth, who are ever indulging in self-admiration, nor one of those people in positions of power who set themselves up as really somebody. Those, Lord, are the proud whom you scatter in the imagination of their hearts, the rich you send away empty.

But Mary's heart and mind were always fixed on you, Father. She was drawn eagerly towards you as the flower is drawn to the sun. All her trust was in you alone. She was ever alert to do your will as a truly humble servant. And that is why you showered your blessings upon her beyond what one could dream of.

It is always those with such dispositions as these that you pick out for preference to carry out your plans for they are completely untrammelled and unattached and there is nothing to impede you from endowing them with your gifts and filling them with your Spirit.

Mary already radiated the spirit of the Beatitudes. Blessed indeed was she who was poor in spirit, who hungered and thirsted for justice, who was merciful, clean of heart and possessed of peace.

Thank you, Father, for giving us Mary as a model of faith and love.

We thank you for giving her to us as a model of what the Church should be.

We pray, Lord, that your Church may not let itself be caught in the trap of the ways of worldly power and the wielding of wealth.

May the Church ever see itself as your "lowly handmaid". May it place all its trust in you and in your word as its supreme, indeed its only, wealth and asset.

Imitating Mary, may the Church not seek worldly power, conquest nor self-enrichment, nor seek to condemn.

May its constant concern be to stand fearlessly, as Christ did, by the least ones of this world, the poor, the ostracised, completely confident that all else is in your safe-keeping, even if that means it must go through Calvary and endure the Cross.

Father, would that I could always say with Mary and with your Church: "Behold the handmaid of the Lord. Be it done unto me according to your word".

Praying at Christmastide

Christmas

"You will find a babe wrapped in swaddling cloths and lying in a manger". (Lk 2,12)

The first Christmas: The world was waiting for the Messiah, one who would be a king and use his kingly power, a judge who would administer justice, a ruler who would wield his power, a legislator who would enact laws. . .

But when he came he was a newborn babe who could only smile and cry, a babe born into poverty, all weak and puny.

That was not what people had been expecting. It did not fit in with their set ideas. We are, they said, not impressed.

Christmas today: The world is looking to the end of a crisis, the end of unemployment. There is plenty of choice food to eat, money, regular rises, success, growth, untouchable privileges, winter sports, time off in spring and summer. . .

We sing of the newborn babe and the stable and how tiny he is and his smiles and his tears.

And that's that.

And off we go to our Christmas dinner and all our fun and games.

But that is not true of everyone. There is a handful of poor shepherds and there are three Magi.

There are always the poor. There are those who scan the heavens and follow a star, those who thirst after justice and peace and the innocent children who love the newborn babe with all their heart.

All these seek him out and draw near and gaze in wonder.

Yes, it is truly he whom we have been waiting for. It is he who will teach us the secret of loving and caring, how to forgive and how to make peace, respect for the least ones and love for those looked down on. He brings hope and joy, the secret of a life well lived, the art of self-giving.

The Word of God

"He is the image of the invisible God".

(Col 1,15)

Lord Jesus Christ, you are the living, spoken word of God.

You express in human terms what God is in his innermost being.

You come to us at Christmas under the signs of poverty, simplicity and love. And in this way you reveal to us the thoughts of God, his preferences, his mind.

You shatter our set way of thinking about what makes a person's worth: not his elated material and financial success, not his pedestal in society, not his influential position or privileges, but a spirit of love and sharing and constant concern for the well-being of others.

Then there is our set way of thinking about God. Father, how wrong we are just to think of you as intransigent, jealously protecting your grandeur and your rights, exacting offerings of sacrifices and blood poured out in expiation for the sins of men. Thanks to Jesus Christ who came to disclose your hidden face, we discover in you a Father providing for the needs of your children, a Father who makes us feel at home, forgiving, reconciling, setting us free, ensuring our happiness and bidding us partake in the universal banquet. A magnanimous God, full of humanity, who wishes to share fully with us.

Lastly, there are out set ideas about religion. Our relationship to you, Father, is not, as we so mistakenly think, simply a matter of rites and ceremonies, but first and foremost a matter of attachment and love.

Christ, our Lord, when you came among us it was to set up a quite new world for us. That world has gone on growing for well nigh 2000 years. But all that time, too, it has been under attack.

Pour into us, Lord, your Spirit of love, of unselfish service, of solidarity with the poorest of the poor whom you love so much.

Teach us to turn our lives into one, joyous, unending Christmas day, that festival of sharing and self-giving for the sake of others.

By your coming amongst us may a new humanity be born and grow up to maturity, that very humanity which you planned for mankind from all eternity together with your Father in the secret of your heart as God.

The Incarnation

"And the Word became flesh".

(Jn 1,14)

An espoused couple are not content to tell each other that they love one another. Their love is a tangible reality.

Neither is God's love for us only a spoken word. The love of God was made flesh. "The Word was made flesh and dwelt amongst us".

He became one of the poor and one of the least ones, so much so that he was ranked with sinners and treated like an outcast.

If my love of God is only empty words ("Lord, Lord, I love you") it is illusion. "It is not he who says, 'Lord, Lord', who enters the kingdom of heaven but the one who does the will of my Father". My love of God must become a tangible reality, "incarnate" in my practical love for others, in positive acts of sharing and solidarity.

"Let us not love in words, but in deeds and in truth".

If the good news is likewise made a mere matter of words, that too becomes illusion. The good news must also become tangible in positive acts; "Go and tell John what you hear and see, the blind receive their sight, the lame walk, the deaf hear and the dead are raised up", Jesus said to John the Baptist's disciples. And St Paul said: "I have become all things to all men."

If, again, the Church is only a mouthpiece it will make no impact on the world. Mere words are just thin air. The Church has to take root in the very substance of human life, right at the heart of the world.

"As you have sent me into the world", said Christ to the Father, "so have I sent them into the world".

Lastly, if my faith is a mere formality and the Creed just a set of words, they are reduced to nothing but theory. Faith and Creed must, like the rest, become incarnate in human life, get to grips with the world, actively and vitally. "Faith without good works is dead"; "faith works through love".

The star

"The star which they had seen in the East went before them. . . When they saw the star, they rejoiced exceedingly with great joy".
(Mt 2,9.10)

Lord, when the Magi looked at the sky it was full of hundreds of brilliant stars. I am left wondering how they chose the very one that would lead them to you.

Today thousands of starry lights blink at us, each beckoning us to take it as our guide. One beckons to effortless satisfaction and pleasure for the asking. Another twinkles with money, comfort and material goods in plenty. Another leads the way to sex, drugs and living at the toss of a coin.

There is the star of service to others, the gift of oneself to suffering. Another spells passion for art or science or politics and power.

And lastly there are all kinds of stars of love that can lead to an enormous variety of patterns of behaviour.

The question is how to choose the right star. They are all tempting in their particular way, especially for young people wondering which way to turn as they begin to wake up to life. But choose one must.

*　　*　　*

Lord Jesus Christ, one day you told the crowds: "No one can come to me unless the Father draws him" (Jn 6,44).

Lord, may your Father make those stars brightest that put us on our way towards you, and especially those that lead straight on to you. May they draw us on, and the young people, too, and all who seek for light to guide their lives.

At another time, a few days before your death, you said to the crowds: "When I am lifted up from the earth I will draw all men to myself" (Jn 12,32).

Lord, draw us to yourself. Draw all men by the shining light of your Gospel of love and peace, your Church, your saints who have followed you wholeheartedly, your Spirit sent upon all mankind and everywhere at work. And grant, Lord Jesus Christ, that our lives may mirror something of your light and reflect it for our neighbours to see, so that like the Magi, they may set out on the path that leads to you.

It was on your cross, Lord, that you were "lifted up from the earth", and yet still more by your resurrection. Draw to yourself all mankind as it journeys through history. May the power which draws all men to yourself bring them ever closer to the end for which you made them, the day when we shall be like you since we shall see you face to face in the fulness of light.

Seeking God

"Those who seek him shall praise the Lord . . .
You who seek God, let your hearts revive".
(Ps 22,26 and 69,32)

The Gospel narrative of the Epiphany contains a tragic contrast. The Magi, who were pagans, are shown seeking for the true God. And they find him. On the other hand the religious leaders of Jerusalem, who held to traditional beliefs, learning that the Messiah had been recently born, just cannot be bothered to go to him and, indeed, in the long run reject him.

*　　　*　　　*

Lord, it is true that the traditional believers amongst us are plentiful. Do not allow me to be lulled into complacent security in my faith as though the fact of believing in you dispensed me from setting out to seek you.

The high priests and scribes in St Matthew's account of the Epiphany reacted as though they were sitting tenants. They reckoned they possessed you, that they were fully informed about you once and for all. They were quite satisfied, had all the answers, as secure as could be in their dogmas and their catechism. They were shackled by their certitude and resistant to anything whatsoever that turned up from elsewhere.

But, Lord, you are not just a doctrine or a definition. You are an identifiable person.

However close we may be to other people — friends, husband, wife, relatives, children — we never get to know one another totally. However much we try there are always some things that remain impenetrable.

If that is true of one human being towards another it is not surprising that for us to get really to know you, Lord, even a little, we need to be ever in your company, not only by thinking things out but even more by turning our hearts towards you.

Lord, help me to set out on my journey as the Magi did and not confine myself to set formulas, the sheer wording of the Creed or the Catechism, for your wonder far exceeds the ablest definition.

If I am to begin to get to know you, I must undertake to follow you right through the Gospel, the way the apostles did, and like them be swept off my feet by the things you say and do, and jolted out of my habitual way of thinking about things. Precious is the time I spend leaving all else aside and think only of you, Lord; for then you become truly central in my life.

I must seek you and find you by thinking about you and contemplating you and opening my heart to you. I must seek you through committing myself actively to follow your example. For the light you give, Lord, is not primarily in the form of learned discussion and subtle notions but is the ongoing outcome of love and living, a light that will break through to me from the good deeds I do for others in imitation of you.

I must seek you, Lord, not in the narrow limits of my own thoughts but in absorbing your thoughts, catching reflections of them wherever I may. You readily make me aware of them by means of the everyday life of people I currently meet and through them, whether they are unbelievers or not, for the "Holy

Spirit speaks to us even through the unbelief in which so many of our fellowmen find themselves today".

Lord Jesus Christ, since you come to seek and save those that were lost, teach me to seek you always, you who are the life and salvation of the world.

"In the streets and in the squares I will seek him whom my soul loves. . . I found him, I held him and would not let him go" (Song of Songs, 3,1–4).

Lord, why is it that you hide away?

"While gentle silence enveloped all things . . . thy all-powerful word leaped from heaven".
(Wisdom 18,14.15)

King David wished to build a temple in your honour, Lord. His motive was of the best, realising nothing could be too splendid for you. And yet you declined his project.

And take Nazareth. The angel came to announce to Mary that she would be the mother of your Son. Yet no one around her knew anything about it, and even Joseph, her betrothed, was not told until later on.

Why is it, Lord, that you hide away when you intervene in the life of mankind?

It was the same at Christmas. You let Christ be born in a stable at dead of night. No one was told it was happening except the few poor shepherds. It is as though you do not realise how we just love anything out of the ordinary and that the crowds only rise to the sensational and the spectacular. After all, publicity does count! And even today you refrain from making a public impact. The signs you give us of your love and your power are never compelling and leave people free to put their own interpretation on them.

*   *   *

God would reply that he recognises all that. But, he tells us, do you not know that my ways are not your ways, my thoughts are not your thoughts? Why should I want that temple from David? The whole universe is my dwelling place. But what I do indeed want is to come and dwell in your hearts and in your lives, to make humanity itself my temple and my home, and that each one of you should be ready to give me a welcome. I want my kingdom to be extended in your hearts and minds.

If you really want to build me something, so be it. Work together to build a world of love and brotherhood, a world which will be a sign of the coming of my kingdom. Give a welcome to the poor and the people of no standing in the world, and the disabled, the blind, the outcasts and the sinners and to all who hunger after justice and love. For all these are precious treasures and it is to them first of all that my kingdom belongs.

Build your life, chip away at the sharp edges and the rugged surface of pretentions, cleanse and purify, make everything clearcut so that my presence may be displayed through you.

Let all you do, however commonplace it may be, all you decide on and everything you undertake bring into the world around you that light the world is for ever looking for.

Then you will find that the signs of my power and my love which you imagine are so low keyed, will seem easier to detect and more striking. For it is you yourselves who must serve as my signs, and so must my Church. "You are the light of the world".

Prayer and the kingdom of God

Signs of the kingdom

"The poor have good news preached to them".
(Mt 11,5)

I am sometimes disconcerted, Lord, by your manner of acting towards me. It is as though you kept hiding in order to make me look for you.

Where would you have me find you? There in the tabernacle in the church? In that little group of people that meets once a month to pray together and experience the happiness of true friendliness? In church on Sundays when we all gather for Mass? In the person of the priest in charge of our parish? In the voice of our Pope? In the quiet of my night prayers?

True enough you are, of course, actively present in all those instances.

Just now I will watch you at work in the Gospel. I see you going from place to place. The crowds constantly swarm round you. There you are, speaking to the people. You let the scribes and Pharisees, who have precious little regard for your teaching, challenge you. You are open to questions from the friends of John the Baptist who himself seems a little taken aback by the way you act. He tells them to ask you: "Are you the one who is to come or must we look for another?"

Your answer opens their eyes. "Go and tell John what you have heard and seen. The blind have their sight restored, the lame walk, the lepers are cleansed, the deaf hear, the dead are restored to life, and the poor have the good news preached to them".

It is out and about in the full beat of life that you want to implant your kingdom and make it grow, and not exclusively in our tabernacles and churches and the hidden recesses of our prayers and the friendly warmth of our gatherings.

It was out in the world at large, Lord Jesus, that you spent your life and that, too, is where your Spirit is at work today.

You are at work, Lord, wherever evil is on the wane, wherever people pull themselves together and go ahead with renewed courage, or wherever people of strong convictions from all kinds of backgrounds get together determined to improve human conditions or wherever there is a move towards unity, reconciliation, peace. Yes, Lord, in all these instances you are present and active.

Your kingdom is already implanted when a married couple who have separated are reconciled with one another again, when starving children are given food and a normal life, when world powers come to an agreement and diminish their armament, when an immigrant neighbour is treated like a brother and is made to feel welcome.

All these things are signs that your kingdom is growing and that your Spirit is renewing the face of the earth. When barriers begin to be dismantled and hands are outstretched and solidarity becomes firm, all this means that you are there.

Lord, give me the ability to see and to hear and to discern the signs of your presence as life goes on around me. Let me walk along with you so that I shall be led wherever you wish me to go, as your Spirit inspires.

Beatitudes

"Blessed are the poor in spirit, for theirs is the kingdom of heaven". (Mt 5,3)

I forget all too easily, Lord Jesus Christ, that your message is essentially good news, a call to happiness.

How is it that we have so often managed to turn it into a message of anxiety and fear and have concealed your face behind a mask of harshness and severity? And to think that on the day you were born the angel greeted the shepherds with: "Do not be afraid, for behold I bring you good news of a great joy which will come to all the people; for to you is born this day a Saviour" (Lk 2,10–11).

And the charter of your kingdom which you came to solemnly

inaugurate comprises eight articles each beginning with the words, Blessed, happy...

But it is not some hollow happiness that you hold out to us. You love us too much to do that. You put us on our guard against turning up blind alleys and pursuing shoddy pleasures that are ever out to beguile and ensnare us.

You want us to have genuine happiness, deep and lasting. That is the happiness you yourself know so well, Lord. For yours was the heart of the poor in spirit, free from all yearning for comfort and wealth. You were truly open-hearted, always approachable and helpful.

You were happy because you were always a total stranger to sentiments of violence and resentment, always motivated by gentleness, compassion and forgiveness.

You found happiness in striking a sympathetic note with others, sharing their sorrows and their joys, moved to shed tears with those who wept.

Your happiness was in thirsting for justice, being a bearer of peace wherever you went, your very own peace and the secret of being at peace amongst ourselves.

Your happiness was in having a heart so pure that you saw the hand of your Father at work in everyone and everything.

Your happiness was to find your nourishment, your complete fulfilment and satisfaction in accomplishing your mission out of love for your Father and doing his will in everything.

Even during your passion, even on the cross, you knew that by your suffering you were giving birth to a new world and a new humanity. Like a mother, her suffering once over, is ecstatic with joy as she holds her newborn babe in her arms.

Your happiness was in giving, even giving your very life for those who are your very own.

It is your desire that your very own joy should be in us and that our joy should be full.

Teach me, Lord, never to be led astray in my search for happiness but always to find the paths that lead to that special joy which is yours.

The salt and the light

"You are the salt of the earth. . . You are the light of the world".   (Mt 5,13.14)

I am sometimes tempted, Lord, to compare your Church with those small shopkeepers who have done precious little to keep up with the times. It has not occurred to them to make their shop windows attractive and the chances are that their merchandise is a bit on the stale side too.

The result is that whereas the elderly folk, set in their ways, still do their shopping there, the younger folk do not find them the least bit attractive and go off elsewhere to find their salt and light.

And yet it so happens that here and now you are telling me: "It is you, my friends, who are the salt of the earth and the light of the world and you, my Church, must be that salt and that light". So the real problem, Lord, is not getting down to giving the "shop" a new look but first and foremost making sure we ourselves are true salt and true light by letting ourselves be stimulated by your Spirit and not allowing ourselves to be carried off by our own petty notions and personal preferences.

Another thing about salt is that you must be able to shake it out of the saltseller onto the food. And as for the light, it is no use leaving the lamp under the table or locked up in the cupboard. It must shine for everyone in the house and all the passers-by.

Lord Jesus Christ, you did not count equality with God a thing to be grasped but emptied yourself and came right into the midst of the world, fully man amongst men, there to be the salt and the light.

Far from standing aloof you went amongst the mass of the lesser folk and the poor, the sick, the lepers without nevertheless neglecting the important people and the well-to-do.

You are the sower who went out to sow the seed. And that seed was nothing less than your love, your word, your smile, your life and blood. And it was all so wonderfully seasoned and glowing with light that it fascinated the crowds. So did you come to transfigure the world as the light of the sun transforms the countryside and brightens up its colours.

Help me, Lord Jesus Christ, to break loose from the make-believe world in which I am for ever locking myself up. Teach me how to be the salt and the light of this world which you have entrusted to me. You are not asking me to overpower the people around me but to be the means of helping them to taste a little of your goodness and see things in your light. It is not a matter of blinding them with light or imposing my ideas and convictions on them but of being full of your Spirit myself and of enlightening those who are trying to find things out and helping them to pick their way as best they can.

Lord, may your Church no longer set me making comparisons with those old-fashioned shops. Let it rather remind me of a tall lighthouse beaming its light round the world and may the mass of your true friends by a myriad of shining lamps lighting up the lives of everyone with confidence and joy.

Love as God loves

"Be therefore perfect, as your heavenly Father is perfect". (Mt 5,48)

Lord Jesus Christ, you invite me to take God himself as my model. But the perfection of God is surely something quite beyond my reach!

Fortunately you have also told us: "I give you a new commandment; love one another as I have loved you".

It ought indeed to have occurred to me. Since you are the perfect image of the Father, modelling oneself on him is modelling oneself on you, loving as you love. And I find signs of your love on every page of the Gospel and every page of my life-story.

You loved the sick and the poor and those children the apostles wanted to send off, and all those who were in one way or another looked down on because they did not belong to the "right set". You were even specially fond of those usually rejected and all those who used to be labelled "sinners".

Your love for them consisted in the first place in regard for them as individuals. Your first approach was not to recruit them or convert them but to help them, to put them securely on their feet, restore to them their human dignity as sons and daughters of God. When you cured or pardoned anyone you did not go on to regimentate them but left them completely free to go their own way. That was the case, for instance, of the Samaritan woman and the woman who was a sinner at the house of Simon the Pharisee and the one taken in adultery and Zacchaeus and so many more.

Teach me, Lord, to love as you loved the most abandoned, the ones that people instinctively shun, and to show my love by attuning myself to them, happy to be treated as they are. There are for instance the foreigners who have come to live here, the handicapped, the youngsters looked on as young hooligans, and it must be said often behave that way. Give me, Lord, the gift of loving them with patience and kindliness and at the same time really succeeding in doing them good.

Teach me to be for them what you yourself would be.

Open my eyes to catch a glimpse of your presence in them, of your Spirit working in them. For you have been loving them long before I came along, and your Father makes his sun shine on them and rain fall on them as on everyone else.

To be perfect means loving as you love, Lord, with a love that extends to everyone and at the cost of a total gift of self.

Living your life means loving like you.

Heaven and eternal life means loving like God.

Risen Christ, teach me to free myself from the bondage of self, so as to embrace your Spirit and come to love like you and be alive with your life.

Confidence

"Do not be anxious about your life".

(Mt 6,25)

Father, what could Jesus Christ really mean when he told us not to be anious about our life and our needs? After all, Father, you have entrusted parents with their families, children and others close to them and you want us to cope with all we have undertaken under the inspiration of your Spirit.

It is you who have given us the task of handling the world. It is you who call on us to bring about peace and build a world in which the underdeveloped countries can meet their needs and where tiny children will no longer be fated to die of starvation.

Jesus says: "Look at the birds of the air . . . your heavenly Father feeds them . . . consider the lilies of the field . . . your heavenly Father clothes them as even Solomon in all his glory was not clothed". But somehow that does not work when applied to us. After all, the birds and the flowers, unlike us, are not beings who can think and take responsible decisions. You do not treat us, your children, as though we were brainless beings, but as beings equipped to make deliberate choices. You have entrusted us with shaping our future and that of our families and children and country and the world at large. What then did your Son mean when he said: "Do not be anxious about your life . . . ?"

The keywords of what he was telling us were still to come: "Your heavenly Father knows that you need it all" (that is, money, food, clothing . . .).

And that is precisely the bit I tend to overlook. I get anxious and worked up as though everything depended on me alone. I keep forgetting that you are my Father, a Father who loves me and never leaves me on my own. I forget that although I must indeed accept full responsibility, at the same time everything also depends on my Father who is always at work with me. And it may well be that when I have decided to do something you may well have cleared the way already to enable me to do it.

You do not reproach me for working away and facing up to my responsibilities. But you do not want me to be keyed up with anxiety, forgetting that my responsibilities are yours as well. They are truly *ours*.

Family, children, work are all our joint concern, yours and mine. So, instead of getting worried about things, I ought rather to talk to you quietly and with absolute trust in you.

"Seek ye first the kingdom of God and all these things shall be yours as well."

Jesus does not even say: "You should worry and fret for the sake of the kingdom of God" but "not even for the kingdom of God...".

You want us, Lord, to seek quietly, unruffled. You yourself, Father, are the kingdom of God, you yourself in me and with me, in our families, in my work and in all my responsibilities great and small.

Teach me, Father, to seek you with quiet self-possession, so as to detect the traces of your presence in my daily round of life, ever open to the influence of your Spirit of fortitude and love, telling you trustingly when things do not work out the way I want, remembering all the time that you love me and that I must never give way to worry, for you are my Father.

The treasure

"The kingdom of God is like a treasure hidden in a field". (Mt 13,44)

A treasure that one discovers hidden in a field?

But, Lord, that kind of thing does not really happen nowadays. It is as though one were to say that the kingdom of heaven is discovered by one person in a million about once every ten years. At that rate one might give up looking once and for all.

But there is just this. A treasure is not necessarily something of great value in itself. It may be something that is precious for personal reasons. Even children have their treasures, a doll, a teddy bear, a box of coloured chalks. You have only to see what a scene they create if you try to take them away. Paltry treasures if you like, but priceless possessions in their eyes.

Come to think of it, Lord, I am no different. I too have my paltry treasures to which I am desperately attached, my car, my social standing, my reputation, the deference people pay me, my comfort, my jewelry. . . Attached! I would sacrifice anything rather than lose them.

But you, Lord, make me see things quite differently. You tell me in so many words that it may be fine to have all those things but does it not rather make me look like one of those little girls so pleased with themselves as they parade their imitation jewelry for admiration from all and sundry?

That amounts to missing the essential for the sake of the accessory. The essential is something quite different, something concealed that escapes notice.

Zacchaeus went out seeking to see you, Lord, and he found you. The crowds sought to touch you as you went about in the villages of Palestine and as a result they were cured. Mary Magdalen went looking for you at the tomb and she found you. In the Songs of Songs the bridegroom sought his beloved and found her.

The kingdom of heaven is not a thing to own; it is yourself, Jesus, who are to be sought after in the way one busies oneself hunting for a treasure.

You are the light of our lives and the light of the world, the "goal of human history and civilisation, the centre of mankind, the joy of all hearts, the fulfilment of all aspirations" (Gaudium et Spes 45).

And we know where we have to look for you — in the Gospel and in the Eucharist, of course, but also in our communion with our fellow Christians, and in the poor of whom you have said "theirs is the kingdom", and in unbelievers, who are our brothers, too, and all who are searching in other ways than ours since you have scattered widely the seeds of truth and love and sometimes people are left to discover for themselves where the seeds have in fact been sown.

Lord, teach me to stop clinging to worthless treasures that mean so much to me, and show me how to break with the unthinking routine I have got into in religious and other matters. Teach me to keep searching until I find you, the true treasure of our hearts, and come to you in a new light in which I see you truly for the very first time.

Praying at Eastertide and Whitsun

Emmaus

*"While they were talking and discussing together,
Jesus himself drew near and went with them".*
(Lk 24,15)

Two men walking along the open road. Two men totally down-cast walking along a cheerless road and pondering the days gone by. Disillusioned, saddened, aimless. It was all over.

"We had hoped...".

Millions of people going down the open road. Millions disheartened, walking in the dark, shrouded in worry, sadness or fear. On a road that leads nowhere, with nothing to look forward to.

A third man comes up and walks along with them. Stranger though he is they feel he is a friend.

Little by little he brings them out of the cloud of depression that envelopes them until it is completely dispelled.

How good it was to talk with this stranger and tell him your fears and anxieties. He listens and understands so well. He helps you to carry the cross. He enlightens and stimulates you and your heart warms to him.

"Stay with us". And in the house comes sharing, conversation, a feeling that they belong together.

Then, the breaking of bread. Their eyes are opened. They see the light. "It is the Lord!"

Soon they are out on the road again. The same road but this time they are stepping out with joy. Everything has come to light. The same road, but now it is leading somewhere. A future lies ahead to be fashioned and knit together.

That other road, with the millions of people walking along it with heavy hearts, walking in the dark, a road that leads nowhere...

Will they one day meet that third man, the stranger who turns out to be the great friend, the Friend who will break bread with

99

them and warm their hearts and set them safely on their journey into the future?

The Son of God crucified

"He is the image of the invisible God".

(Col 1,15)

Lord Jesus Christ, from the moment of your birth you have been the image of the invisible God, by your silence, your discretion, your closeness to us and even your physical weakness and your poverty. For it was out of love that you came, and that means letting those you love set the pace and adjusting oneself to their poverty and weakness as one keeps them company.

Thanks to you we become aware that God is not first and foremost the All-powerful but the All-loving, considerate, humble, kindly, caring.

All through your missionary life, Lord, you bore this resemblance to your Father, in healing the sick, cleansing lepers, raising the dead, inspiring hope. In your pardon of Zacchaeus and the reception you gave the Samaritan woman you showed clearly, as in all your actions, the true nature of the good news.

You were the perfect image of your Father, for the teaching you gave and the works you did were his. As light of the world and resurrection and life you reflected him.

It was perhaps on Calvary that you bore still more clearly this perfect resemblance to the invisible God, for there your love for us is shown to the very end. You were there nailed to the cross between two criminals, insulted by one of them, derided by the chief priests.

Humiliated, broken, rendered powerless, you lost nothing of your inner freedom and it was freely that you gave your life out of love. There could be no more perfect expression of the infinite love of your Father for us. "No greater love has a man than this, that he give his life for his friends".

For the Father, as for you, Lord, to live is to love and give yourself unsparingly. You died as you had lived, loving to the utmost.

Lord Jesus Christ, we too have been created to the image and likeness of God. But we allow that image to be tarnished.

Thank you, Lord, for reminding us how we can make it shine again so that you perceive in us the brothers and sisters of your beloved Son.

Disfigured and transfigured

"He was transfigured before them".

(Mk 9,2)

Lord Jesus Christ, your face was disfigured by the blows, sweat and spittle and the crown of thorns.

And we have disfigured the face of humanity which you wanted so much to create to the image and likeness of God.

It is by our lack of love, our pride, our intolerance and our violent actions that we disfigure and defile it.

We disfigure it when we stand by unmoved as penury and injustice reduce the lives of our brothers to a sub-human level.

We disfigure our own faces when we give way to fear and discouragement and doubt. Then ours are faces with panic and distress written on them.

But you, the risen Lord, show at this season your face transformed in glory. And you call us to share this transformation in our lives.

Help us to shed our doubts and fears and be reborn to faith and trust, whatever may occur. May your smile transform our faces and your love transform our lives.

Help us to be reborn to the love of our brothers and sisters. The very fact of loving changes our lives, brings resurrection and willing transformation.

Teach us to be like you in sharing the life of those around us, the life of the neighbourhood where we live.

Teach us to master our timidity and to get involved with such competence as we possess in changing the face of the world that is marred by fear and depression.

Every time we impart a little love and confidence and joy

where there has been bitterness and dejection we are on the way to transforming both ourselves and the world.

But that double transformation, Lord, is above all the work of your Spirit who renews men's hearts and the whole of creation. The universe and humanity are here and now being transformed until at length there will be new heavens and a new earth.

Lord, may we welcome your Spirit of love and renewal as year by year we greet the coming of spring and the new face of nature that it brings.

Easter: passing over

"Arise, my love, my fair one, and come away".
(Song 2,10)

Right through our life, Lord, we are constantly moving on, from one day to the next, from season to season, year to year, child to grown-up, adult to old-aged. There is marriage and sickness, joys and trials. And we shift from one house to another, one kind of work to another, sometimes amounting to a total change.

In creating us you did not mean us to remain inert but to live and grow, be creative, build, explore and progress and renew ourselves constantly.

The word Pasch, incidentally, means "passing on". There is for instance the Pasch of the Hebrew people. They moved on across the Red Sea and through desert. They went from the land of death to the land of the living, from slavery to freedom. They discarded the outlook of the slave who does everything out of fear for that of the free man who follows his own conscience.

Lord, I must always have that Pasch in mind, for my own sake and for the sake of others. For you call all of us to free ourselves from every form of slavery, oppression, penury, injustice, and from slavery of our own making like pride, wealth, sensuality.

Teach me, Lord, to be a free man, to follow the voice of conscience enlightened by your Spirit.

Help me to be concerned for those of my fellowmen who, left to themselves, fail to be free.

Then, Lord, there was your own Pasch. Knowing that your hour had come, the time to go from this world to the Father, having loved your own you loved them to the end.

It was your total commitment to love that led you to go forward to Calvary, the cross and death, and on to the resurrection. And this Pasch you accomplished entirely of your own free will.

Your resurrection was not a reversal, a return to earthly life, but a transition to the life of God.

You did not shed your humanity when you went through death and rose again; you did not reject your body as though it had become a thing of no further use. On the contrary, you entered whole and entire into the eternal life of God. From then on our human nature has a place in glory.

We, too, each one of us, have our Pasch, Lord Jesus Christ, thanks to your own.

Thanks, indeed, to your own Pasch, for you are the One who uniquely go before us. It is thanks to you that death is no longer an impasse nor a relapse into non-existence. Far from it, it is a new and lasting birth into that eternal life for which we were created. It spells unending freedom and rest where we shall enjoy in your company, Lord, the complete fulfilment of all our aspirations beyond anything we could ever have imagined.

There we shall find everything that is beautiful, love without limit, total truth, transparently clear communication between ourselves and others, in a word, life to the full.

Lord, teach me to see my death not as an end to everything, an utter void, but as the last stage in reaching my goal, the crowning of my whole life.

Since then this final Pasch means passing through death, as you have done, Lord, I must prepare for it by all the decisions I make and all the choices I settle for day by day.

Every day there are countless minute "paschs", moving constantly on from egoism to a habit of concern for others, from intolerance to kindliness and understanding, from domineering to being of service to others.

Thanks to these minute "paschs" I foster my growth and

steadily transform myself, or rather, your Spirit transforms me, Lord, and fashions me to your likeness. By stifling the seeds of death in myself and freeing myself from everything that shackles and paralyses me, I unite myself with your death to go forward with you to the risen life.

Lord, make me alert to all those small "paschs" with which I must daily make my way, for my own sake and for the sake of the world around me.

How true to say "not only for my sake but for the sake of the world in which you have placed me", Lord.

For the whole world aspires to its eternal Pasch. The entire universe yearns for the time when at long last it will have a share in the freedom and glory of the children of God. It is now in the pangs of childbirth but with the hope of coming at last to its final transformation. "The world passes away", says St John. The life of the risen Christ is already active in it like yeast in the dough. The universe is going forward towards "a new heaven and a new earth". Eternity has already begun. When you come in your glory, Lord Jesus Christ, we shall appear with you in full glory and the whole universe with us.

Come, Lord Jesus!

The meaning of life

"He is not God of the dead, but of the living; for all live to him".   (Lk 20,38)

Lord God, Jesus has told us to call you "Father". A father is one who gives life and sustains it.

My parents were instrumental in giving me life but it is from you that I received it, Father, you the original source of all life.

It is in you that I "live and move and have my being", as St Paul said.

"It was you who created my being, knit me together in my mother's womb. . . My being held no secret from you when I was being fashioned", as is written in the Psalms.

With St Paul I can say that you have chosen me in Christ before the creation of the world, to be holy and undefiled in your sight.

So, Father, I am conscious that if my life belongs to me it is because it has been given to me by you through my parents. I did not acquire it of myself. It is you who have entrusted it to me, with all its resources of health, intellect, steadfastness, and abilities which I have to put to good purpose.

It is all mine and yet it all comes to me from elsewhere and it is all beyond my comprehension. I cannot claim to be the absolute proprietor of this life of mine. And I am equally conscious that my life, coming as it does from elsewhere, is also destined to go elsewhere.

It was not a meaningless gift with no purpose behind it. You gave it to me for a precise object and meaning me to make good use of it. I am not entitled to do just what I fancy with it or squander it. I have to develop it in everything it has. Not one of my talents must remain unprofitable. My heart is designed to love and serve, my mind to think, my strength of will to reach out beyond myself, my health and physical strength to be productive, to work and embellish the world and mankind.

And despite the indignities of old age or sickness, the day of my death will not mean decline and annihilation but rebirth, a bounding forward to something entirely new, a fulfilment I cannot begin to imagine.

Then, Lord, like a kindly father you will wipe away the tears from my eyes and I shall be with you and you will be God-with-me. Emmanuel: God-with-us.

Our attachment will be total, our knowledge without limits and there will not be the slightest hindrance in communicating with one another. Then, Father, you will be in all and in each one love will reign.

Then there will be such joy in loving and understanding and in discerning such an unexpected wealth of things in the people I thought I knew so well here on earth. And no man will be able to rob us of any of this joy.

Truly, Father, you are not the God of the dead but of the living.

Pentecost:
Lord, send us prophets

"The wind blows where it wills, and you hear the sound of it, but you do not know whence it comes or whither it goes; so it is with every one who is born of the Spirit". (Jn 3,8)

I get anxious, Lord, about the future of your Church.

We pray for priestly vocations and do all we can to echo your call "Come, follow me". But we have the feeling that we are saying our prayers and making our appeal in something of a vacuum.

A large proportion of the clergy are around sixty years of age. Recruiting is not all that easy.

As we look at the Old Testament, Lord, we see that a major role was played by prophets who were not priests. You called them, Lord, and endowed them with your Spirit. Thanks to them your sinful people were constantly led to do penance and return to you. It was thanks to them that the people in exile kept up their hope and faith pending their return to their country. Thanks to them also the "remnant" of your people came into being, a poor and humble little group filled with your Spirit. Mary of Nazareth was to be one such; she who was the mother of Jesus Christ your Son.

In the face of the shortage of priests today, Lord, send us "prophets": men and women filled with your Spirit, people who will not be put off by the difficulties they meet but will go ahead, ranging over a wide field that stretches even beyond the boundaries of the visible Church. Let them be intelligent people, knowledgeable and forthcoming, able to grasp the situation of today's world and able to speak its language, people with an eye for the kind of world that is shaping for the future and approaching it with hope and with faith that can move mountains.

I firmly believe, Lord, that your Spirit is at work in the Church and in the world. It has, right down the centuries, enlisted untold numbers of men and women of all walks of life: St Vincent de Paul, St Teresa of Lisieux, Mother Teresa, Martin Luther King, Pope John XXIII...

And how wonderful it is that your Spirit has suscitated so much courage, charity and self-sacrifice both within the Church and in other religions and in the great cultural movements.

So, Lord, I earnestly pray, may your Spirit enlist today men nurtured by the Gospel, and whatever their own original milieu or class may be, dedicated to the poor and needy, to do your bidding whatever the rough and tumble it may entail; men who are not afraid to rouse us from our slumbers.

The essential thing is, if I have grasped Christ's message rightly, that your kingdom, Lord God, may germinate and grow everywhere. That does not necessarily mean exclusively bringing people into the membership of the institutional Church as such. What it does unmistakably mean is promoting the New World which Christ came to launch.

So, Father, raise up prophets in your Church. And raise them up, too, in Islam, Hinduism, in the Marxist world, and in every region of the world, so that all may contribute to bringing your light and your life.

Thanksgiving

"Blessed be the God and Father of our Lord Jesus Christ, who has blessed us in Christ with every spiritual blessing". (Eph 1,3)

Lord Jesus Christ, you did not come first and foremost to suffer and to teach us to suffer and to die, but to love and to teach us to love, so that we might have life and have it more abundantly.

Neither did you come to exhort us to be resigned to evil and suffering, but to bid us combat against them in union with you.

And you did not come to proclaim a Gospel of good news that would only take effect in a world to come after death. It was good news for here and now, calling us to build up our world anew, making it a world of love and peace.

You did not come to reveal a God waving a miraculous wand to waft away our allocated tasks, but a fatherly God calling us to work away at our lives and a God whose love we can always count on whatever may happen.

H

Lord Jesus Christ, beloved Son of the Father, you did not come to divide people up into categories — "good", "bad" — but in order to heal and save and unite all the scattered children of God into one body in your kingdom.

You came to make a new and eternal covenant with all of us, one which nothing can ever destroy. You came to seek and gather together the lost sheep, not in order to confine them in a sheepfold segregated from the world, but so that they could come and go and be the salt of the earth, the light of the world and live life fully.

You came to make free men of us and you call us to genuine freedom; that same freedom which led you to love to the end and give your life for your friends.

Lord, you are the way which leads us to the Father and in the process enables us to discover the true meaning of our life, for we are made for you.

You are the truth, whole and entire. Anyone who loves and labours and seeks to understand the very nature of beings is making his way towards you, even if he is not aware of it.

You are life itself, new life, full of vitality. You call us to be born again. You are the open door, the source of true life. You give your life. You nurture your life in us. You are the bread of life.

Lord Jesus Christ, you came to bring us the water of life, to baptise us, to immerse us in your Spirit, so that our minds might be completely steeped in it and our lives pulsate with it.

You came to bring fire on the earth, the fire of your Spirit, the flame of your love, so that the whole world might be kindled, refined and transformed.

Lord Jesus Christ, you are the light of the world. You came to enlighten all men so that none might remain in the darkness and that we might walk in the light and become "children of the light".

The whole world is seeking you. And all those who are living in the love of their fellowmen, living in communion with one another, these have already found you.

You are the sun shedding your rays on all mankind, the joy of all hearts, the one on whom all man's desires converge.

Blessed are you, Lord Jesus Christ!

Returning to the Lord

The priestly prayer of Jesus

"Father, the hour has come".
(Jn 17,1)

Lord Jesus Christ, let me make my own the thoughts that filled your heart and mind on the evening of Holy Thursday as you prayed the priestly prayer which the apostle John records in the Gospel.

All through that prayer your thoughts turn to the Father and to your disciples. It is as though your very existence is absorbed in him and in the mission he entrusted to you. Everything you do and say is to do with him and with us. You live, not you, but your Father lives in you and speaks and acts in and through you. And all this is done out of love for him and for us.

In that prayer the word "give" occurs no less than seventeen times: the Father has given everything to you and you in turn give us everything. The Father is the fulness of giving. And in that his glory is achieved.

And you, Lord, who are that gift and glory of the Father, find your own glory in giving yourself fully to us and un-reservedly to your mission.

You are truly the image of the Father, the manifestation of love, the perfect expression of the inexpressible God.

To know you is to know the Father.

To know you and the Father is to discover life, that true life to which you call us.

God is love and you, Lord Jesus Christ, and the Father are a loving gift, so that we cannot come to know you except by way of our hearts. We cannot find true life except in love and self-giving. Unless we love both you and the Father, Lord, we cannot know either you or the Father.

Lord, may that affective knowledge, that insight of the heart enjoyed by those absorbed in love, ever grow in me.

But it must be said that in that evening at the Last Supper a special thought dwelt in your mind. Soon you would no longer be visibly present amongst your disciples. How would they cope with their mission? Your mission was on the brink of completion and you were about to leave this world into which the Father had sent you.

As for your disciples you were about to send them on their mission in the world. There was no question of taking them out of the world for they could only carry out their mission if they were firmly planted in it, but without ever succumbing to its way of thinking. This would be no easy task.

You warned us what would happen. In running counter to the spirit of the world whose only creed is wealth and creature comforts, violence and deceit, it will turn its hatred on us, despise us and persecute us.

Lord Jesus Christ, you prayed to the Father to safeguard us from the spirit of the world, just as you had safeguarded your first disciples from it. You prayed for us that whatever our trials might be we might always have your joy in us.

Never allow us to succumb to fear, nor let it prevent us from taking our stand by the destitute, nor reduce us to being a tool for those who wield money power, or becoming the minions of any kind of political power.

Do not allow your Church to become paralysed or to opt for silence for fear of being persecuted. Lord, make us totally dedicated and immovably anchored in our loyalty, whatever may happen, just as you were in your loyalty to the Father, even in the face of death.

Lord Jesus Christ, that evening at the Last Supper, your "hour" which you had been waiting for so long, your thoughts were focussed on one ultimate attainment, the accomplishment of the Father's plan for mankind, namely, that we might all be one as you and the Father are one. As you are one in him, so should we be one in you.

And may this come about without delay so that the world may know that it is the Father who has sent you, and that it may believe and have life.

Then when, despite our many differences of race and culture, we achieve that perfect unity, you in us as the Father is in you, and then the world will recognise it as the outcome of the Father's active love. Lord, teach us this love. Lift us above our divisions and absorb us in this unity. Then we too shall be close to the final hour or, rather, on the brink of the first moments of the New World. That is your supreme wish, that all of us should be gathered together with you and contemplate your glory. That we should possess the fulness of life and of happiness, that we should share together in the infinity of your love and the love of the Father and that we should find in you our fulfilment for all eternity.

Father, thy kingdom come!

The Lord's second coming

"Come, Lord Jesus".

(Rev 22,20)

"As in the days of Noah they were eating and drinking and marrying and giving in marriage . . . and did not know . . ." (Mt 24,37). They were going along day by day with never a thought for where it was all leading.

God our Father, that is how it is today. They eat and drink and get married without bothering about the meaning of this life of ours. They rise in the morning, go off to work, come home again and off to bed, day after day.

Spring, summer, autumn, winter come and go and the year starts all over again. People are born, grow up, reach old age and die. Others follow on with the same round of life. We live as though life consisted of going round and round on the same unvaried course and as though human history consisted in constantly coming back aimlessly to the same starting point.

Thank you, Father, for having revealed to us the meaning of life and the meaning of the history of mankind. Far from going round and round in an aimless circle, we are going onwards into a purposeful future, on towards a renewal and to someone waiting for us.

That "someone" is none other than Jesus Christ, your Son, who has come already and is to come again. "He will come again in glory . . . and his kingdom will have no end".

He has come already to show us how to live and love as he does and to sow seeds of his kingdom in this world of ours. For you wish, Father, to bring all your scattered children together

111

in him, so that they may find their fulfilment in unity and love.

And it is in expectation of this that you would have us live, and it is this that you would have us strive to foster. That means breaking down the barriers that divide us and learning to respect and love one another.

The day will come when Jesus Christ, your Son, returns to set the seal on his kingdom, the final transformation of the world.

Clearly then the history of mankind is not like a helmless ship or the plaything of blind destiny. No, we have a clear-cut purpose; we are on the way to a fully satisfied fulfilment, to an everlasting springtime, where love and peace will reign.

And all that will be the work of your hands. And yet it is your wish that we too shall be involved in accomplishing it.

Father, with your help may I make Jesus Christ at home at every moment of my daily life, so that I may be ready to welcome him when at last he comes again in glory.

Come, Lord Jesus! We await your coming!

Heaven. . . ?

"In my Father's house are many rooms . . . I go to prepare a place for you . . . I will come again and will take you to myself, so that where I am you may be also". (Jn 14,2.3)

I am saddened, Lord, at the way people distort your message. But after all, the fault may lie with us, because it is our mission to make your message known to those around us.

An unbeliever once said, "You people who believe in God are like children who just do what they are told because they know they will get something nice in return. So you behave properly because you expect to enjoy heaven when you die. Compare that with me", he said, "I do what is right purely from a sense of duty, not for personal gain".

Then there is that good old soul who tells me in a hushed whisper that, after all, resigning oneself to suffering is the done thing. One has to suffer, doesn't one, so as to get to heaven?

And there is the youngster who says: "All this talk about a promised heaven means absolutely nothing to me. Happiness for me means doing things, having a job, battling on, going flat out for success. And once I've got what I was out for, I go after something else. Happiness doesn't consist in possessing something, and certainly not in resting on your laurels. Happiness is actually chasing after something, the sheer joy of the struggle".

Lord Jesus Christ, let me hear you saying once more: "I come that they may have life and have it more abundantly".

Living that life abundantly will mean for me what people mean when they talk about heaven.

Heaven is like a flower that finally comes to full bloom thanks to the warmth and light of the sun. And coming out into bloom is not a reward or a relaxation or something to make up for being previously confined in the bud, but the achievement, the very thing the bud exists for. It does not get there because it has done something to merit it, but precisely because it had the benefit of the rays of the sun, thanks to which it developed perfectly into a beautiful, colourful, sweet smelling bloom.

As for me, heaven will mean achieving my full development as a human being, and I know full well that I can only ever do that thanks to you, Lord Jesus Christ, who are the sun of the human race, for the Father created me in and for you. Without you I would ever be deprived of that eternal dimension of my existence which is my destiny and without which I would remain for ever unfulfilled.

For me, heaven will not be a kind of retirement with nothing to do but relax, but a state of intense and expanding activity, for I shall be immersed in the life and activity of God, like being in a limitless ocean which you can never finish exploring.

Heaven then will be for me the fulness of life and joy and truth, beauty, purity and, along with that, fulness of love, for to live, Lord, is to love.

Heaven will mean total, universal, limitless love. It will be the full flowering of all the attempts at practising love, kindliness and giving of self that I have made during my life in this world, imperfect and limited though they may have been. In heaven I shall find all my relatives — parents, children, brothers and sisters — and everyone I have known and loved here, as well as friends, neighbours, fellow-workers. And then there will be those who really never meant anything to me and even people I never knew at all. We shall all be bathed in perfect, transparent love, uniting all of us in endless happiness.

But above all else, Lord, heaven for me and for all of us will be you yourself; we in you, as you yourself are in the Father.

Heaven will not be a thing or a place. It will be you yourself because, as you yourself have said, you are the way, the truth and the life, you are the light that draws us like a beacon and the spring of water that satisfies our thirst. You are the bread which alone can satisfy our hunger for purity, beauty and love.

Heaven will be at long last finding our Father, seeing him face to face, for we shall see him as he is. And delight in finding him will extend throughout eternity.

Heaven will be seeing the fulfilment of his plan for all creation, the great gathering together of all the nations, races, peoples and tongues, and the joy of having played our little part in the realisation of that plan.

Lord Jesus Christ, I find that the best image of the joy of heaven is the happiness of loving spouses. Their happiness does not come as a recompense but is part and parcel of their love itself, and if one were to ask them what reward would please them most, they would simply say to be able to love one another still more, because, they would explain, love for them means everything.

Heaven, Lord, will be the happiness of loving you and the Father in the Holy Spirit. And nothing will ever be able to harm this love, and nobody will ever be able to rob us of it.

And God's joy will be all in all

"These things have I spoken to you, that my joy may be in you, and that your joy may be full".
(Jn 15,11)

God is love. And what does love disclose?
God is life. And what is life in action?
God is joy, joy in loving, joy in giving, joy in relating to others, joy in making all things fruitful.

Think of God's joy as he looks at creation and sees the whole universe, the product of his creative word and filled with his Spirit. "And God saw that it was good".

God's joy at light and life and the countless beings great and small, the sea and the mountains, winter and spring, the flowers and the harvest. "And it was all indeed good".

God's joy over men and women created to his image and likeness, made to love and be loved.

God's joy over the love fiancées have for one another, a love that springs from his own love, happiness which is a reflection of his own happiness. Joy at the promises they make, modelled on the promises he made to the chosen people.

God's joy at the birth of a babe and the love lavished on it, the infant making its first steps and just beginning to say "mama" and "dada", the smile of the little girl, the mystery of adolescence, the charm of the young woman, the tender care of a mother, the physical fitness of a grown man, the playful twinkle in an old man's eyes.

God's joy at having created men and women as his co-operators for the continuance of his creative work and to shape the earth and the universe the way they think.

God's joy when the world is beautified and the human family expands, civilisation develops or man masters the globe and its hidden secrets and even outer space.

God's joy at the use man makes of his intelligence and his labours and at the marvels he produces, from the first tentative tasks of the apprentice to the machines of all kinds that make life easier, from the first little drawing a child offers to its mother to the great masterpieces of painting or monuments or cathedrals.

God's joy when he sees the deepening of friendships and the spirit of fraternity and mutual help and solidarity with the poor, reconciliation, justice and peace.

God's joy at man's efforts to promote the development of nations and the well-being of all concerned.

God's joy at man's festivities, family parties, country fêtes, sports meetings and art exhibitions, all of which bring God's children happily together enjoying themselves and sharing common interests.

God's joy at Jesus Christ, born of the Virgin Mary of Nazareth and supreme masterpiece of creation and the highest perfection of humanity: "You are my Son, my beloved. You are my full joy".

Jesus Christ, God's perfect image, splendour of his glory, radiance of his love.

God's joy at being, through Jesus Christ, the light of mankind, the way of life, the bread and the power of resurrection.

God's joy at healing, forgiving, setting people on the right path and renewing hope and trust. "There is more joy in heaven over one sinner doing penance than for ninety-nine just. . . It was fitting to make merry and be glad for your brother was lost and is found".

God's joy in gathering his people together and saving mankind. "The Lord your God gives you victory . . . he will rejoice over you with gladness . . . he will exult over you with loud singing".

God's joy in renewing the covenant and extending it to all mankind. "As the young bride gives joy to her husband, so shall you give joy to your God".

God's joy at Jesus Christ revealing the secret of happiness, his very own happiness to which he calls his children. "Blessed are the poor in spirit, blessed are those who weep, blessed are the meek, blessed are those who hunger and thirst after justice, blessed are the pure of heart, blessed are the peacemakers, blessed are those who are persecuted for justice sake. It is more blessed to give than to receive".

God's joy at Jesus Christ welcoming the lowly, the poor, the sinners, the lepers and all kinds of outcasts, taking their side and making them the first to hear his secrets. "Jesus rejoiced in the Holy Spirit and said; 'I thank thee, Father, Lord of heaven and earth, that thou hast hidden these things from the wise and understanding and revealed them to babes; yea, Father, for such was thy gracious will' ".

God's joy at the Church made up of weak men and women who are sinners and who, in spite of that, struggle on to promote Christ's cause in time and space.

God's joy in sharing his life with the countless baptised people and in stimulating so many people from all races and religions who willingly absorb his Spirit.

God's joy in his hopes that his plan will be achieved and life and happiness will bossom once the pangs of childbirth and the waywardness of man are overcome and the wheat grain has been well and truly buried in the ground and taken root.

"When a woman is in travail she has sorrow . . . but when

she is delivered of the child she no longer remembers the anguish for the joy that a child is born into the world. So you have sorrow now, but I shall see you again and your hearts will rejoice and no one will take that joy from you".

"God will wipe away every tear from their eyes and death shall be no more, neither shall there be mourning nor crying nor pain anymore, for the former things have passed away".

"These things I have spoken to you that my joy may be in you and that your joy may be full".

And God's joy will be all in all!